10

MINUTE GUIDE TO

MICROSOFT®
EXCHANGE

by Gabrielle Nemes

QUe®

A Division of Macmillan Computer Publishing
201 West 103rd St., Indianapolis, Indiana 46290 USA

©1996 by Que® Corporation

International Standard Book Number: 0-7897-0677-6

Library of Congress Catalog Card Number: 95-72562

98 97 96   8 7 6 5 4 3 2 1

Interpretation of the printing code: the rightmost number of the first series of numbers is the year of the book's printing; the rightmost number of the second series of numbers is the number of the book's printing. For example, a printing code of 96-1 shows that the first printing of the book occurred in 1996.

Printed in the United States of America

Publisher Roland Elgey
Vice President and Publisher Marie Butler-Knight
Editorial Services Director Elizabeth Keaffaber
Publishing Manager Barry Pruett
Managing Editor Michael Cunningham
Development Editor Seta Frantz
Production Editor Phil Kitchel
Copy Editor Paige Widder
Cover Designer Dan Armstrong
Book Designer Kim Scott
Technical Specialist Nadeem Muhammed
Indexer David Savka
Production Team Brian Buschkill, Joan Evan, Trey Frank, Amy Gornik, Michelle Lee, Kaylene Riemen, Michael Thomas, Kelly Warner

Special thanks to Discovery Computing for ensuring the technical accuracy of this book.

CONTENTS

INTRODUCTION

So you want to send a message to your coworkers in the next building, across the campus, in another state, or in the Hong Kong office. Microsoft Exchange's e-mail is the communication tool to use. No paper, no busy signals, no voice mail!

Want to send a fax copy of that great looking ad layout you're working on? Use Exchange's Fax Services! The fax machine resides right on your desk, in your own computer, in fact.

Need to explain your thoughts about the latest revision of the budget? No problem—send a message back to the boss and include your spreadsheet full of changes.

Need to work at home this week? Simple. Use Exchange's Dial-Up Networking and Remote Mail functions to quickly connect to your computer at the office.

Have to get everyone together? Use Schedule+ to check their calendars, schedule the meeting, and reserve the meeting room. Easy!

These common functions represent just a few of the powerful features available to you on your own desktop computer using Microsoft Exchange. The *10 Minute Guide to Microsoft Exchange* will get you started. Fast!

WHAT IS THE 10 MINUTE GUIDE TO MICROSOFT EXCHANGE?

The *10 Minute Guide to Microsoft Exchange* is a quick and easy guide to learning the most important features of Exchange. Short, concise lessons, each about 10 minutes or less in length, give you step-by-step instructions. If you've never used Microsoft Exchange, start at the beginning and work through each lesson. After you've finished the first eight or nine lessons, you might consider skipping around, picking those lessons which cover those tasks you'll use immediately.

As you proceed through the book, you'll see three important icons:

 Timesaver Tip icons present quick and simple suggestions for faster methods of completing a task.

 Plain English icons define computer and Exchange terms which may be new to you.

 Panic Button icons will help you out of areas where users often get into trouble.

Conventions Used in this Book

Using a computer, especially one with Windows 95, which requires use of both a mouse and a keyboard, can sometimes present challenges when attempting to describe just what to do. Therefore, the conventions listed below are used:

Select Using the mouse, point and click a choice from a list. Your choice will usually be highlighted, indicating that it has been selected.

Check/Uncheck Click the mouse in a checkbox which appears in a dialog box to mark or unmark an option.

Choose Using either the mouse or the keyboard to make choices from a menu.

In addition, you will see these conventions:

Items you select Items you select, or keys you press, appear in color.

Key combinations   To use some keyboard instructions you must press a combination of two or three keys, such as "Press Alt+T" or "Alt+Shift+T." When you see these instructions, press and hold the combination keys (Alt, Ctrl, Shift) while you press the last key. Then release all the keys.

Shortcut keys   Shortcut keys appear in bold color. They correspond to the underlined letter which appears on many buttons or menus in Exchange. You can usually use a shortcut key by pressing Alt+*shortcut key*.

FOR FURTHER REFERENCE

If you're new to Windows 95, be sure to review Appendix B for some important pointers. In addition, you might find it useful to also refer to these books:

10 Minute Guide to Windows 95   by Trudi Reisner

The Complete Idiot's Guide to Windows 95   by Paul McFedries

Easy Windows 95   by Sue Plumley

ACKNOWLEDGMENTS

Of course, I owe a big thanks to my family for carrying on with life while I locked myself in a room to write. And a special thanks is due to all of the helpful people at Que for their suggestions and advice. Thanks everyone!

WELCOME TO EXCHANGE

In this lesson you will learn the purpose of Microsoft Exchange. You will also learn the difference between Exchange for Windows 95 and Exchange Server.

WHAT IS EXCHANGE?

Microsoft Exchange provides information services based on messaging. Exchange enables you to perform tasks, such as sending and receiving e-mail or faxes. You can manage personal calendars, create to-do lists, and schedule group meetings. You can even design custom applications and forms with Exchange.

Exchange refers to each of these tasks as *information services*. One definition for information is meaningful data. In other words, it's data on which you can act and make decisions. Entries in your appointment book are more than just text, they are information. You decide whether to go to a meeting scheduled in your appointment book, or ignore it.

The method you use to share information between co-workers, friends, or other computer users is referred to as *messaging*. You can send messages by conventional means such as talking directly with someone, by sending a letter using the U.S. Post Office, by courier such as Federal Express, or by leaving a voice mail message on a telephone system. Exchange uses an electronic form of messaging referred to as e-mail. It's by far the most efficient method.

UNDERSTANDING THE EXCHANGE VERSIONS

Exchange comes in two flavors—the version that installs as part of Windows 95, and the full-blown version, called Exchange Server. This book is primarily about Exchange for Windows 95 which, in future chapters, will be referred to as "Exchange." You probably only use one version, but be sure to review the sections for both versions since important concepts are presented in each.

WHAT IS EXCHANGE FOR WINDOWS 95?

So what, exactly, comes with Windows 95 Exchange? The Windows 95 Exchange piece is a small version of the full-blown Exchange Client. It is included with Windows 95. It does not, however, get installed by default when Windows 95 is installed. (See the inside front cover for installation instructions.)

Windows 95 Exchange gives you just a portion of the full Exchange Server application. While it is often referred to as the Windows 95 Client, you do not have the same complete functionality that is available when you are using the Client portion of the Exchange Server.

Windows 95 Exchange by itself is a powerful application which allows you to easily communicate with other users. It allows you to create and manage e-mail with one Postoffice. You can manage, send, and receive faxes directly with your own computer. You can connect to The Microsoft Network, as well as compose, deliver, and receive e-mail with The Microsoft Network. More information on The Microsoft Network can be found in Lessons 19 and 20. Unlike Exchange Server, Windows 95 Exchange does not allow you to create and manage an appointment book or data-entry forms without additional software.

Some component parts of Exchange Server can also be individually purchased, such as Schedule+ and the Microsoft Mail Server. These will be discussed where appropriate.

Windows 95 Exchange by itself is a powerful application which allows you to easily communicate with other users. It allows you to create and manage e-mail with *one* Postoffice. This means that you can send or receive e-mail from persons in your immediate network or workgroup.

You can also send or receive e-mail from online services such as The Microsoft Network, CompuServe, GEnie, America Online or other message services. If you have a fax modem, you can compose, send, and receive faxes.

You can attach files and objects created from other applications to your messages or faxes. You can organize your messages in logical folders. To keep your messages organized, Windows 95 Exchange helps you maintain address books and message folders.

If you work away from your office, Remote Services will allow you to dial up your network to send and receive messages. You can even schedule Exchange to automatically pickup or deliver messages at specific times during the day!

Even without Exchange Server, Windows 95 Exchange allows you, if you desire, to create a Postoffice on a network server. This gives all users the ability to share a common Address Book which maintains the e-mail address for each person on the Postoffice.

You do not need a network to take advantage of some of the more powerful features of Exchange, however. If you're not on a network, your Postoffice and Mailbox resides on your own hard drive. An installation of this type is often referred to as a *stand-alone* system.

On a stand-alone system equipped with a fax modem, you can exchange mail with other users of online services, such as The Microsoft Network. You can also send and receive faxes with your own computer. In addition, you can use Remote Servers, as described in the preceding paragraphs.

WHAT IS EXCHANGE SERVER?

Exchange Server consists of two modules, or pieces: the Server module and the Client module.

A server is usually a central computer which controls the activities of a network (a group of computers connected in some fashion). The server is usually loaded with software that is shared by everyone on the network. Often, the server also stores files (such as documents or spreadsheets) so that they can be easily edited, opened, or accessed in some fashion by everyone on the network.

The server portion of network software usually controls the larger, and shared, activities. For example, in Exchange Server, the Server module controls the actual delivery of messages to each user's computer. To clarify, suppose that you want to convey a message to your co-worker, Joe. You compose the message, address it to Joe, then send it. The message first goes to the Postoffice which resides on the server. The *Postoffice* is a common location where all users have individual Mailboxes (just like the U.S. Post Office). Because the Postoffice is central to all users, your message to Joe can be efficiently routed and transfered to Joe's Mailbox. This process is called delivering the message.

 Send and Deliver   Send and deliver are two entirely separate processes in both the Exchange Server and in Windows 95 Exchange. Send is the final step in composing a message. **Sending** a message stores it temporarily at the Postoffice. The Postoffice **delivers** the message to your recipient's Mailbox on a regular schedule (usually every 10 minutes or so) or when the recipient requests that all mail be delivered. More information on sending and delivering messages can be found in Lesson 5.

The Client module of Exchange is used and installed on each individual computer. Client modules contain a subset of the complete software package and are not shared with other users. Client modules let you perform as much of a task as possible without going back to the server for instructions. Client/Server applications are considered to be more efficient simply because most of the application is processed at the client workstation.

For example, the Exchange Client module allows you to create and send a message. Exchange Client can't deliver the message by itself. That job belongs to Exchange Server, which organizes all incoming and outgoing messages and then delivers them to the correct Mailboxes.

To carry this one step further, Exchange Server runs only on Windows NT. It manages multiple Postoffices and can transfer messages between many other mail systems. Included with Exchange Server is Schedule+, a calendar and scheduling application. Schedule+ allows you to create and manage appointment books, to-do lists, and contact lists. It also allows you to schedule meetings.

Exchange Server also includes Microsoft Exchange Forms Designer, a forms and applications designer. Forms Designer allows you to create data-entry forms such as expense reports, timesheets, and so on.

Finally, Exchange Server includes enhanced e-mail security features, such as digital signatures and fax encryption. Very simply, *digital signatures* provide a secure method of signing a message, attachment or fax. *Fax encryption* is a method of protecting a fax from being read by persons who do not know or have not been given the right to read or open the fax. An encrypted file cannot be read unless it is unencrypted.

Exchange Server is compatible with a variety of platforms and network types, such as Novell Netware, Internet, CompuServe, and AT&T. Exchange Clients are available for computers which run Windows 95, Windows 3.1, Windows for Workgroup, and DOS.

In this lesson you learned the purpose of Microsoft Exchange. You also learned the difference between Exchange for Windows 95 and Exchange Server. In the next lesson you will learn how to start and stop an Exchange session and how to complete the Inbox Setup Wizard.

STARTING AND QUITTING EXCHANGE

In this lesson you will learn how to start and stop a session with Exchange. You will learn how to complete The Inbox Wizard, how to attach to your Postoffice and Mailbox and to enter your password.

STARTING EXCHANGE

There are two possible methods used to start Exchange. However, before you can start, Exchange must be installed. Review both starting methods listed below. Then if you aren't able to start Exchange using one of the methods, you can assume that it has not been installed and you must do so. To install Exchange, refer to the inside front cover of this book for installation instructions.

STARTING EXCHANGE FROM THE DESKTOP

The easiest method to start Exchange is to double-click the Inbox icon on your desktop as shown in Figure 2.1. If installation of Exchange was fully completed, the Exchange Viewer will appear. If installation was not completed, the Inbox Setup Wizard will start. For help completing the Inbox Setup Wizard, refer to the inside front cover, beginning with step 4.

FIGURE 2.1   The Inbox icon starts Exchange from the Desktop.

STARTING EXCHANGE FROM THE START MENU

If the Inbox icon does not appear on your desktop, you can also start Exchange from the Start menu using these steps:

1. Choose Start.

2. Select Programs.

3. Choose Microsoft Exchange.

If the installation of Exchange was fully completed, the Exchange Viewer will appear. If not fully completed, the Inbox Setup Wizard will begin.

COMPLETING THE INBOX SETUP WIZARD

A *wizard* is a tool in Windows 95 that guides you, step by step, through an application's installation and setup process. The Inbox Setup Wizard guides you through the setup steps for Exchange. The information you complete for the Inbox Setup Wizard is stored in a *profile*. It is normally completed at the time Exchange is installed. The Inbox Setup Wizard, therefore, will only appear if it was not completed at the time Exchange was installed, or if your profile does not exist or is damaged.

Profile The Exchange profile contains your personal preferences for working with Exchange, such as a list of the information services you use, the name of your Postoffice and Mailbox, and your password.

Because the Inbox Setup Wizard will appear differently depending on the information services you have available, the steps listed below are general, rather than specific, to each individual possibility. You can easily edit a profile at a later time if you make a mistake while completing the wizard or if you do not know or cannot find the necessary information. You can also add or remove services at a later time.

Before you complete the Inbox Setup Wizard, you must know some important information:

- You must know the name and path of your Postoffice.

- You must know the name of your Mailbox.

- You must know your password. (The default password is "PASSWORD.")

To complete the Inbox Setup Wizard, follow these steps:

1. The Inbox Setup Wizard starts by displaying a list of the information services which have been installed. Check the services you want to use. Some services are essential to Exchange, such as Microsoft Mail, the Personal Folders and a Personal Address Book and will appear automatically on the list. Any other services you've installed will also appear on the list.

   If you want to use services which do not appear on the list, such as CompuServe or The Microsoft Network, you must install them. Figure 2.2 illustrates a commonly used information services list. See Lesson 21 for information on adding services to your profile.

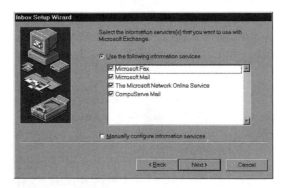

FIGURE 2.2   The list of installed information services appears in the Inbox Setup Wizard.

Remote Session
last 2 boxes checked

MSN-Properties
1ST & 3rd box checked

Delivery —
Personal Folder
none
Microsoft Fax Transport
Microsoft Mail on c:\Windows\WPGD
The Microsoft Network Online Service

Path to Post OFFICE

C:\WINDOWS\WGPO\

LOGON

MAILBOX

no password

box checked for auto. enter.

delivery

both boxes checked (at top)

Remote Conf.

1st 2 boxes checkd.

2. Now follow steps 6-12 of the installation instructions for Exchange that appear on the inside front cover of this book. See Lesson 22 for more information about creating a personal profile.

ATTACHING TO YOUR POSTOFFICE AND MAILBOX

When Exchange is installed and started, the MS Mail logon dialog box will typically appear (see Figure 2.3). Although it might not appear if only one profile exists on the current system, or if you have previously told Exchange to use a default profile and to remember your name and password.

FIGURE 2.3   Starting Exchange may require completing the Microsoft Mail Logon screen.

To complete the Logon screen, use these steps:

1. Verify or complete the name of your Postoffice and Mailbox.

2. Type your password. For security, the password will appear as a series of asterisks (****). If you make a mistake, backspace and retype your password. If your password is incorrect, you will have three more attempts to type it correctly. After the fourth try, Exchange will start in offline mode. Offline mode allows you to compose and send messages. But they'll not be delivered, nor can you receive messages, until you successfully connect, or attach, to your Postoffice.

3. Check the Remember Password check box so that you are not required to type your logon information each time you start Exchange.

Offline Mode The option to work in offline mode only appears when you normally work in a network or workgroup setting. When you are logged on to your network, you are said to be "online." Conversely, when you are *not* logged on, you are "offline." The same terms are often used when you work with online services such as The Microsoft Network. When you are connected by phone line, you are "online." When not connected, you are "offline."

Forget your password? See your system or MS Mail administrator if you don't remember your password.

4. Choose OK. The Exchange Viewer appears.

EXITING EXCHANGE

There are two methods to quit Exchange. You can:

- Choose File, Exit. When you exit, the Exchange Viewer will close. You will not receive messages or faxes until you start Exchange again and log on. Your Postoffice will still be accessible using other mail products.

- Choose File, Exit and Log off. When you exit and log off, Exchange will close and so will any other *group-enabled* application such as Schedule+. Similar to Exit, you will not receive messages or faxes until you start Exchange again and log on.

Group-Enabled   A group-enabled application is one that allows you to share information between users. Although it is not strictly necessary to do so, Exchange is designed to be a network or workgroup application. It allows you to share information—it is group-enabled.

If you Exit, or Exit and Log off, you will not be notified of any incoming mail, nor will you be able to receive faxes until you start Exchange again. It's a good idea, therefore, to leave your Inbox open by not exiting until the end of the day.

In this lesson you learned how to start and stop a session with Exchange. You also learned how to complete the Inbox Setup Wizard and how to log on. In the next lesson you will learn how to work with The Exchange Viewer.

EXPLORING THE MAIL SERVICE

In this lesson you will learn how to work with the Exchange Viewer, how to display your folder list and folder contents, and how to modify the size of the Exchange Viewer and the width of each column. You will also learn the purpose of each of the default Toolbar buttons and how to customize the Toolbar.

THE PURPOSE OF MICROSOFT MAIL

Microsoft Mail is the central product for Exchange. Using MS Mail, you will compose, format, send, retrieve, reply and forward e-mail messages to persons on your network or for whom you have installed an information service.

THE EXCHANGE VIEWER

The Exchange Viewer is the primary screen you will use in Exchange. It appears automatically when you start Exchange. It displays the folder list, the contents of each folder, the Toolbar and the status bar. All of the messages you create in MS Mail are managed from the Exchange Viewer.

When started for the first time from the Inbox icon, the Exchange Viewer will display the contents of the Inbox (the list of messages you have received). If you first start Exchange by choosing Start, Programs, Microsoft Exchange, both the Inbox and the folders list will appear (see Figure 3.1). When you restart Exchange, the Exchange Viewer will display using the view settings from your last session.

Status Line   Folder List   Inbox   Toolbar   Column Header Buttons

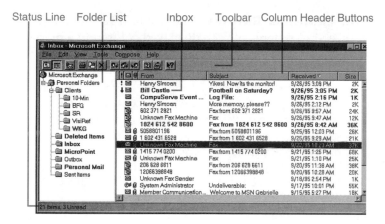

FIGURE 3.1   The Exchange Viewer can display both the Inbox
and the folders list (here shown with added folders).

Folder List   The folder list displays all of the folders in
which messages are stored. Think of a folder as a named
container in which you store, or keep, messages. Four folders
are automatically created when Exchange is installed: the
Inbox (which lists messages you receive), the *Outbox* (which
lists messages that have not yet been delivered), the *Sent
Items* folder (which lists messages that you sent), and the
Deleted Items folder (which retains messages you delete from
any other folder).

Folders and subfolders that you create will also appear in the
folder list. Subfolders help you further organize your messages. Collectively, all folders are referred to by Exchange as
your Personal Folder service. Lesson 10 will help you create
folders and subfolders.

Inbox   The contents of the Inbox are automatically displayed when you first start Exchange. Messages to you are
delivered to your Inbox.

Toolbar   The Toolbar contains buttons which start frequently used tasks. The default Toolbar buttons are listed
later in this lesson under the heading "Toolbar Buttons."

Column Header Buttons   The Column Header Buttons identify the contents of each displayed column in a message header.

 Message Headers   Messages listed in any folder will display the name of the person who sent the message, the subject line of the message, and the date and time the message was sent. Additional columns can also be displayed as part of the message header. You can learn how to do so in Lesson 22. The combination of these items is called the message header.

Status Line   The Status Line lists how many messages are stored in the currently displayed folder and how many of those messages have not been read.

VIEWING THE FOLDERS

When Exchange is installed, a Personal Folder service is set up and configured with four subfolders: Deleted Items, Inbox, Outbox, and Sent Items.

The four default folders are used by Exchange as follows:

Deleted Items   Messages that have been deleted from another folder are stored in the Deleted Items folder.

Inbox   All messages which you receive appear in your Inbox. The Inbox folder is automatically open when you start Exchange and is, therefore, the *default* folder view.

Outbox   Messages that have been sent, but not yet delivered, reside in your Outbox. On a network, however, the messages fly so quickly through the Outbox to the server that they often cannot be "caught in flight" in the Outbox.

Sent Items   Messages that have been delivered appear in the Sent Items folder.

Want to further organize your messages? You can add new subfolders, sometimes referred to as "sibling folders," to help organize your messages and files. Subfolders are folders created *inside* other folders. It might help to think of subfolders as dividers inside a school binder. The binder is the folder. The divider further organizes the papers within the binder. Subfolders further organize messages within a folder. For more help on creating folders, see Lesson 10.

Why have folders? Using folders allows you to logically organize your messages or other files. Before you can open another folder so that you can see its contents, you must view the folder list. To view (or hide) the folder list, follow these steps:

1. Choose the View menu.

2. Choose Folders. The folder list displayed in Figure 3.2 contains both the default folders and some custom folders.

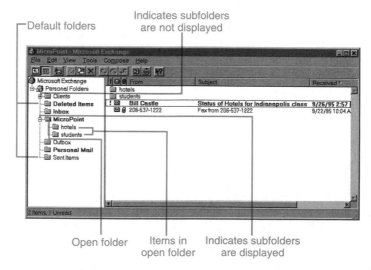

FIGURE 3.2 The folder list.

Hiding the Toolbar and Status Bar   The View menu is also used to display or hide screen elements such as the Toolbar, Status Bar, or Folders List. Choose View, then click the screen item you want to hide. Click the item again to display it.

Displaying the Contents of Each Folder

The contents of the Inbox folder is usually displayed when you start Exchange. To view the contents of any other folder:

1. Verify that the folder list is displayed. Choose View, Folders if it is not.

2. Click the folder icon to open it and display its contents. If subfolders exist, click the plus (+) or minus (-) icons to open or close the subfolder display.

If you have a long list of messages, or if your message header text is longer than you can comfortably view, resize the Exchange dialog box by dragging one of its sides or corners.

You can also adjust the width of each of the message header columns. To do so:

1. Place the mouse pointer over a button edge on the Column Header button bar. You will see a double-headed arrow.

2. Drag the mouse pointer to adjust the width of the column (see Figure 3.3).

3. Release the mouse when the column is the desired width.

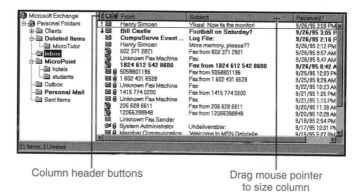

Column header buttons   Drag mouse pointer
to size column

FIGURE 3.3   Drag the edge of a Column Header button to adjust column width.

USING AND CUSTOMIZING THE TOOLBAR

The Toolbar buttons provide a quick method of performing common tasks. You use a Toolbar button by clicking it with the mouse. You can get quick identifying help for each button by viewing its Tooltip. Tooltips display briefly below each button to identify the button's purpose (see Figure 3.4). You can see a Tooltip by pointing to each button on the Toolbar (let it rest there briefly).

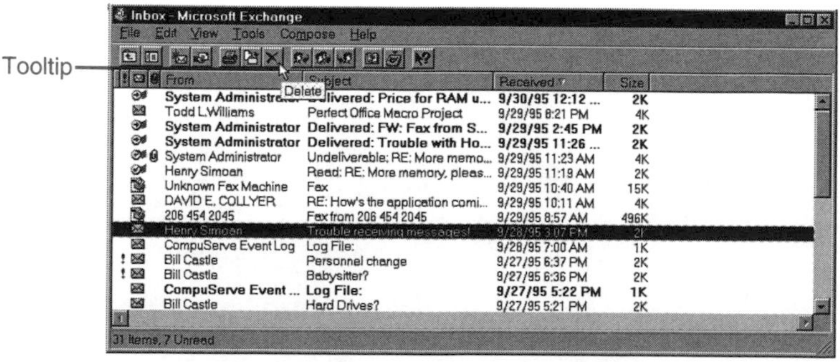

Tooltip

FIGURE 3.4   Tooltips will briefly appear when pointing to a Toolbar button.

The Toolbar is dynamic. Each button on the Toolbar is specific to the activity being performed in Exchange at the current time. For example, if you are sending an e-mail message, the Toolbar will display buttons specific to sending e-mail messages. If, on the other hand, you are sending a fax, the Toolbar will contain buttons which help you send faxes.

In this lesson you learned how to work with the Exchange Viewer and folders. You also learned the purpose of each of the default Toolbar buttons and how to customize the Toolbar. In the next lesson you will learn how to use the Exchange Help feature.

GETTING HELP IN EXCHANGE

In this lesson you will learn how to work with the Help available in Exchange. You will discover how to locate help using Help topics, the Contents list, the Index, and the Help Find command.

The Help text for Exchange is a full-fledged reference manual. I like to think of it as an encyclopedia—it's logically organized into topics, there's a table of contents (called the Contents tab), and an index (called the Index tab). But it's one better than a printed encyclopedia because you can search the Help text for specific words or phrases, then display Help text for the Help topics found.

Unlike the unified Help system for Windows 95, where Help for all subjects is combined into *one* Help file, Help for Exchange is split into specific help files for each information service you have installed. For example, when Exchange is installed, Help files are also installed for Exchange and for Microsoft Mail. As you install new services, the Help text for those services will also be installed. Therefore, if Microsoft Fax Services or The Microsoft Network are added, Help files will be added to the Help menu for Microsoft Fax Services and The Microsoft Network.

You can see a list of the Help files which are associated with your installed services by choosing Help or by pressing F1. The Help files appear as items on the Help menu.

You can work with Help using a number of different techniques: The Help Select button (also called the Help, What Is? button) is designed to display text about a chosen screen element. After selecting a Help file from the Help menu, you can, similar to a printed manual, open Help to a specific chapter, then look for information within that chapter. You can also look for help by using the Help Index. The Find function of Help allows you to search Help text for word or word combinations.

Help also uses a technique called *hyperlinking* to connect related help subjects. You can click on a hyperlink (identified with a broken-underline or listed in the See Also section) to *jump* to related Help text.

HELP BASICS

Using Help for Exchange is similar to using Windows 95 Help. To get help, follow the guidelines below:

1. Choose the Help menu. The list of Help files will appear.

2. Select the Help file you want to use. The Help file will open.

3. Select the method you want to use to locate your Help topic by clicking the Contents, Index, or Find tab (each tab is described below). A list of Help topics appears.

   Contents Tab   The Contents tab displays a list of Help topics grouped by sections, or "chapters," similar to a table of contents in a book.

   Index Tab   The Index tab displays a list of indexed words and phrases from which you can choose to display Help text. Help Index is similar to an index which appears in the back of a book.

   Find Tab   The Find tab allows you to search through a *database* (a list of every word in the help text) for a word or phrase you want to find.

4. Select the Help topic you want to view from the resulting list.

5. Read the Help text. The words which have broken under-lines (called hot spots) display pop-up definitions, and those with a solid underline jump to related topics.

Words that jump to other, related topics are called *hyperlinks*. Pop-up definitions open a small window within the help topic you are viewing. Close a pop-up definition by clicking outside it. You can jump to a related topic or read a definition by clicking the hot spot.

6. Close your Help session by clicking Cancel or by clicking the Windows Close button (the little X button in the upper-right corner of the dialog box).

While using Help you can:

- Locate Help topics using the Content, Index, or Find tab.

- Read the displayed Help text.

- Display pop-up definitions by clicking on words or phrases with a broken underline.

- Jump to related Help topics by clicking on words or phrases which contain a solid underline, by clicking the Related Topics button, or by clicking on subjects listed in the See Also section of a Help topic.

- Return to a previous Help screen in the same Help session.

- Write personal annotations to the Help text.

- Copy Help text to the Clipboard.

- Print all Help topics.

- Change the font size used to display Help text.

- Force Help text to remain on top of any other open windows while you continue working.

- Use the Windows 95 system colors for Help display.

See Figures 4.1 and 4.2 to locate Help components.

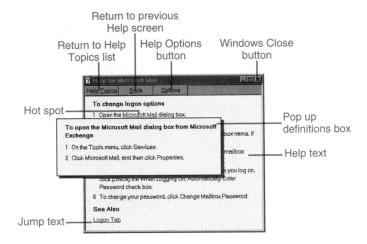

FIGURE 4.1   Sample Microsoft Mail Help Screen.

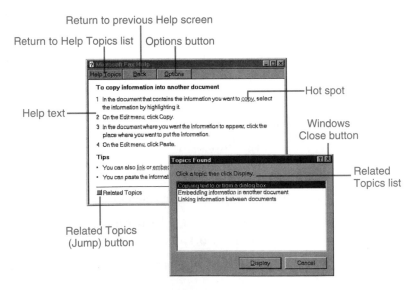

FIGURE 4.2   Sample Microsoft Fax Help Screen.

USING THE HELP BUTTON

The Help button is designed to be a direct method to find help for a specific function represented on-screen. Presumably, you can click on the Help button, then click on anything shown on the Exchange Viewer. For example, you should be able to click the Help button, then click somewhere in the folder list to display Help text about the folder list. Unfortunately, the Help text you receive may or may not directly apply to the item on which you clicked.

Depending on the position you click when using the Help button, you will see one of two screens: an intermediate Help text which directs you to "Common Exchange Functions," or the Help Index.

To use the Help button use these steps:

1. Click the Help button on the Toolbar. The mouse pointer will change to the Help pointer (see Figure 4.3).

2. Click the screen object for which you need help.

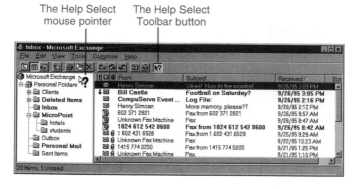

FIGURE 4.3   The Help Select Toolbar Button.

In this lesson you learned how to work with the Help function of Exchange. You also learned how to locate help using Help files and topics. In the next lesson you will learn how to create, format, send, and deliver an MS Mail message.

SENDING A MESSAGE

In this lesson you will learn how to compose and send a Mail message. You will learn how to format the message text, how to set message sensitivity, and how to request a delivery receipt.

Sending a message to someone is similar to writing and mailing a letter. You must know the name and address of the person to whom you're writing, and, of course, actually write the letter. You then put the letter in the mailbox (send the letter) for later delivery by the mailperson (in this case by Exchange). Just as with written mail, conventions exist regarding the appearance of an Exchange address. One great advantage to e-mail is that Exchange doesn't take days to deliver letters like the U.S. Postal Service.

COMPOSING A MESSAGE

The Microsoft Mail Wizard prompts you to complete each step necessary to send a message to persons in your mail network. Composing a message is started using the following steps:

1. From the Exchange Viewer, choose Compose. Then choose New Message (or use the shortcut key Ctrl+N). You will see the New Message - Microsoft Exchange window as shown in Figure 5.1.

2. To address the message, click inside the To text box, then type the name for the person to whom you are sending your message. You can alternatively click the To button and choose a name from one of your address lists. More information about addresses and using address lists is available in Lesson 11. You can address the same message to several people by typing each name in the To or Cc boxes. Separate each name with a semicolon (;).

Type subject here   Type Message text here

Send button   Address areas   Toolbar   Formatting Toolbar

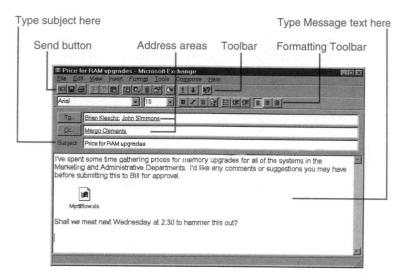

FIGURE 5.1   The New Message dialog box allows you to address and type the text of your message.

Address   A message address can be as simple as a Microsoft Mail address, or as complex as an Internet, CompuServe, or America Online address. Mail can be sent to a variety of mail systems and additional information about addressing mail to other systems can be found in Lesson 11.

3. Press Tab or click in the Cc (**c**ourtesy **c**opy) box. If you desire a copy of the message to be sent to another person, type that person's name.

TIP   **Automatic Name Look Up**   If you don't know how a person's name appears in your address book, you can type the first few letters of the name, then press Ctrl+K to ask Mail to look up the name(s) for you.

I don't know the recipient's name! If you don't know the recipient's name or address for the message, or if the name you looked up wasn't found, you can also find the name entry in one of the address books. See Lessons 11-13 for help in using the address lists.

4. To type the subject line, press Tab or click in the Subject box. Then type the subject line of your message. The subject text you type, while optional, will appear in the recipient's Inbox to identify your message.

5. When you have completed your subject line, click in the text area or press Tab. Now type the text of your message.

You can add a Bcc area to your message by choosing View, Bcc Box while in the New Message window. Then complete the name and address information just as you would for To or Cc. Addressees in the Bcc areas will also receive a copy of your message. However, the Bcc names (and the fact that you even included a Bcc) will not be revealed to recipients in the To or Cc list.

FORMATTING THE MESSAGE

Similar to most word processing software, Mail allows you to "dress up" your messages by formatting the text.

Formatting Formatting, called Rich Text Formatting (RTF) in e-mail, allows you to apply typesetting features such as bold, underline, italics or even colors to your text. You can also use text "layout" features such as bullets or indents, or align text with the left margin, right margin, or center text between the margins (justification).

While you can use RTF in your message text, you should not do so if your message will be sent using Internet or one of the other online services such as CompuServe. These services do not support RTF. Consequently the recipient of your message will not be able to read your message.

If you do choose to format your message text, the formatting can be added to your message either as you type the message or after the message text has been created.

FORMATTING AFTER YOU'VE TYPED THE MESSAGE

To add formatting after you have typed the message, follow these steps:

1. Drag the mouse pointer over the text to be formatted.

2. Click the button in the Formatting Toolbar which represents the attribute you want to use. You can add several attributes to the selected text by clicking on each button you need. See Table 5.1 to view the functions of each button.

3. Click again outside the text to deselect it when formatting is complete.

TABLE 5.1   THE FORMATTING TOOLBAR BUTTONS

ICON	PURPOSE
Arial	The Font List Box. (You can type a font name or pick it from the drop-down list.)
10	The Font Size List Box. (Type a font size or pick one from the drop-down list.)
B	Turns on/off **Bold**.
I	Turns on/off *Italic*.
U	Turns on/off <u>Underline</u>.

ICON	PURPOSE
	Turns on/off a Color from its displayed color list.
	Adds a bullet • to the beginning of each paragraph.
	Decreases indenting (removes an indent) for the current paragraph.
	Increases indenting (adds an indent) for the current paragraph.
	Turns on left justification (each line of text is aligned at the left margin).
	Turns on center justification (each line is centered between the margins).
	Turns on right justification (each line is aligned at the right margin).

FORMATTING AS YOU TYPE YOUR MESSAGE

Adding format instructions as you type the message uses similar steps:

1. Click the button or buttons which start the format instruction you want to use. For example, click the Bold button to start bold. You can click several buttons to turn on several attributes.

2. Type the text to be formatted.

3. Click the buttons again to turn off the formatting.

SENDING THE MESSAGE

When you have finished composing your message and are satisfied with its format, it is time to send the message. To send the message, click the Send button in the toolbar or press Ctrl+Enter. See Figure 5.1 to locate the Send button. The message will then be sent to your Outbox.

 Message isn't in the Outbox! If you are sending a message to someone on the same network and same postoffice you are, the message "flies" through the Outbox faster than you can watch it. The message will automatically be sent to the Mail postoffice awaiting delivery and will appear in your Sent Items folder.

DELIVERING THE MESSAGE IMMEDIATELY

Messages are delivered to each postoffice based on the settings for your personal profile. By default, Mail will deliver messages to another user in your postoffice every 10 minutes. If you also use Remote mail or online services such as CompuServe, those delivery schedules can be individually set up in their respective service properties' dialog boxes. More information about setting or changing properties for other services is covered in Lessons 18, 20, and 22.

You can force MS Mail to immediately deliver your messages and, at the same time, "pick up" any messages for you. To use the menu system to immediately deliver messages, use the following steps:

1. Choose Tools.

2. Choose Deliver Now Using. If your profile only contains the Microsoft Mail service, you will see Deliver Now.

3. Choose the e-mail service you want to use to deliver the message. You can alternatively *poll* for messages to or from all mail services by choosing All Services or by pressing Ctrl+M.

Poll   A method for controlling channel access in which the central computer continuously asks or polls the workstations to determine whether they have information to send.

Shortcuts for Immediate Delivery   If you know the shortcut key assigned to the immediate delivery function you want to poll, you can use it rather than going through the menus. The shortcut keys will vary depending on the number of services you have assigned to your profile. To view your list of shortcut keys, choose Tools, Deliver Now Using. The shortcut keys will appear on the right side of the resulting menu.

SENDING A PRIVATE MESSAGE

Mail allows you to set *sensitivity* levels for your mail. Sensitivity will apply to either new messages or replies you send.

What is Sensitivity?   Sensitivity tags a message with the chosen sensitivity level. It does not hide, password, or encrypt a message in any fashion. The only way you will know that a message has a sensitivity level other than Normal is to add the Sensitivity column to your folder's column display. You will learn about displaying columns in Lesson 22.

To set the sensitivity level for your messages, use these steps:

1. Choose Tools, Options.

2. Click the Send tab.

3. Select the sensitivity level you desire by opening the Set sensitivity drop-down list and highlighting your choice. Select from these options:

Normal   No sensitivity level appears in the column list.

Personal   Personal messages typically have nothing to do with business topics. The word "Personal" will appear in the sensitivity column.

Private   Private messages cannot be modified when re-plied to or forwarded. The word "Private" will appear in the sensitivity column.

Confidential   Confidential messages will display the word "Confidential" in the sensitivity column.

4. Click OK to return to the folder list.

5. Compose your message and send it.

How Do I Know my Message Was Received or Read?

You can ask MS Mail to return a message to your Inbox when your message is either delivered to or read by its recipients. Prior to sending a message use the following steps:

1. Choose Tools, Options.

2. Click the Send tab.

3. Click the checkboxes that indicate that you want a delivery receipt or a read receipt.

4. Click OK when your choices are complete. A receipt will now be returned to your Inbox for each message you send.

In this lesson, you learned how to compose, format, send, and deliver a message. You also learned how to set message sensitivity levels and how to be notified when a message is delivered or read. In the next lesson, you will learn how to locate and read your messages. You will also learn how to sort the message list.

FINDING AND READING A MESSAGE

In this lesson you will learn how to locate, select, open, read, and close your messages. You will also learn how to sort a list of messages.

LOCATING A SPECIFIC MESSAGE

Messages to you are delivered to your Inbox. You can determine which messages have not been read, the type of message received, and whether the message contains any attachments by observing the icons and font type of the messages in the list (see Table 6.1).

TABLE 6.1 **ICONS AND FONTS IDENTIFY MESSAGE ACTIVITY.**

MESSAGE ICONS	INDICATE
Bold	Unread messages appear in bold
Normal	Messages you have read appear in normal text
	Delivered mail receipt
	Returned mail
	Read mail receipt
	Mail Message
	Fax Message
	Urgent Message
	Low Priority Message
	Message has attachments

SELECTING, READING, AND CLOSING A MESSAGE

You can read messages in any folder. However, you will generally want to start by reading your new messages. To do so, use these steps:

1. Display the folder list (review Lesson 3 if necessary), then click the Inbox folder.

2. Scroll through the message list until you see the message you want to read.

3. Double-click the message to open it or select the message and press Enter. The message will open, displaying its contents, and a message Toolbar as shown in Figure 6.1.

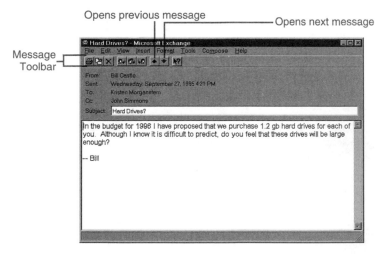

Opens previous message ———————— Opens next message

Message Toolbar ———

FIGURE 6.1   An opened message displays its contents.

4. When you have finished reading the message, click the Close button.

Reading the Next or Previous Message While reading a message, you can quickly move to the next or previous message in your folder by clicking the Next or Previous buttons in the Toolbar or by pressing Ctrl+> or Ctrl+<.

USING FIND TO LOCATE A MESSAGE

It never fails. Just as soon as you think everything's completely organized, you can't find anything. At least in my office. The Find command comes in handy on days like that. Use Find to help you locate a message or file which is stored in an Exchange folder, somewhere.

To use Find, follow these steps:

1. Choose Tools, Find. Or press Ctrl+Shift+F. The Find dialog box appears, as shown in Figure 6.2. As you complete this dialog box, (using the remaining steps) you will select the location to be searched, then define the items to be located.

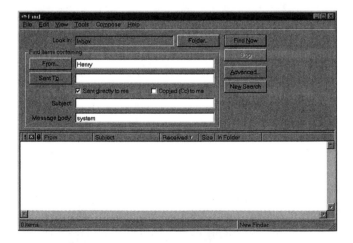

FIGURE 6.2   The Find dialog box helps you locate misplaced messages.

2. Select the folders you want to include in your search. To select a folder, click the Folder button, then select the folder you want to use (see Figure 6.3). If you want to also search subfolders, click the Include all subfolders checkbox. Click OK to return to the Find dialog box.

 Search everywhere! You can include all folders in your search by choosing Personal Folders. Be sure the Include all subfolders checkbox is checked.

Click here to highlight the folder you want to search.

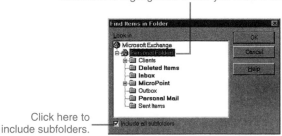

Click here to include subfolders.

FIGURE 6.3 Choose a folder for your Find condition.

3. Complete the conditions to be used in the search. You can set specific conditions for one or all of the fields in the Find items containing section. As you define more conditions, your search becomes more specific. The Find items containing section allows you to choose from the following Find conditions:

From Messages must be from the sender you enter here. You can either type in the name of the sender or, by clicking the From button, select a name from an Address Book. You can enter only a portion of the sender's name, such as the first few letters or a first name. In this fashion, Find will search for all messages where the sender's name *begins* with the characters you typed.

TIP

Messages from me! To find messages you have sent, type your own name in the From box.

Sent To Messages must be to the recipient name you specify here. You can include multiple recipients by separating each with a semicolon (;).

Sent directly to me Messages must include your name in the To box to meet this criteria.

Copied (Cc) to me Messages must include your name in the Cc box to meet this criteria.

Subject The message must include all or a portion of the subject you designate.

Message body The message must include the phrase or text you type in this field. If you want to look for multiple phrases or text strings, separate the strings with a semicolon (;).

4. Click the Find Now button.

In addition to setting general Find Conditions, you can narrow your search even further by using the Advanced Button.

To use the Advanced Find conditions, follow these steps:

1. Click the Advanced button from the Find dialog box. You will see the dialog box shown in Figure 6.4.

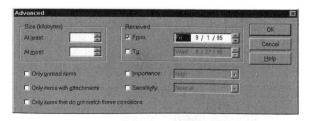

FIGURE 6.4 Advanced Find options narrow your search.

2. Complete the advanced criteria you want to use. You can use these choices:

Size (kilobytes)   The Size section limits the Find response to messages that are larger or smaller than the size range you specify. If the message size column does not appear in the resulting find list, click Cancel from the Advanced dialog box, then choose View, Columns. Choose Size from the field options. (You can add other columns to the display using these steps, also.)

Received   The Received section limits the Find response to messages which fall between the From and To dates you enter. Clicking the checkboxes allows you to enter your date range.

Only unread items   By checking this box, you tell Find to limit its search to messages which you have not read.

Only items with attachments   This box limits Find to those messages which contain attachments.

Only items that do not match these conditions   This returns a display of messages found which do not match any of the conditions you entered. For example, if you have entered a message size range and then check High Importance, messages will be displayed that do not fall within the message size range **or** are not of High Importance.

Importance   Find looks for messages which meet your requirements of High, Normal, or Low importance. Choose the importance level by checking the box and choosing from the drop-down list.

Sensitivity   Find searches for messages which are of Normal, Personal, Private, or Confidential sensitivity. Choose the sensitivity level by checking its box and then choosing from the drop-down list.

3. Choose OK to return to the Items From dialog box.

SORTING THE LIST OF MESSAGES

Sorting the display can help you quickly find the specific message you want to read. You can sort any message display list. To quickly sort the list, click the button which heads the column to be sorted. The list will rearrange in ascending order by that column. Ctrl+click the button to rearrange the list in descending order. Alternatively, you can right-click a Header button to select a sort order from the pop-up menu. A small triangle will appear on the column button to indicate its sort order (up arrow for ascending order and down arrow for descending order). See Figure 6.5 for an example of a list sorted in descending order by date received.

Click on these buttons to sort the columns.

Triangle indicates sort order. In this case, descending.

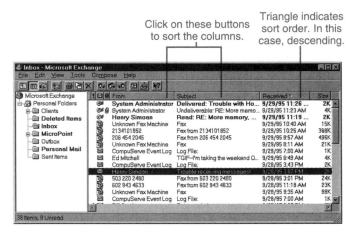

FIGURE 6.5   A list of messages in descending order by date.

In this lesson you learned how to locate, select, open, read, and close your messages. You also learned how to use the Find command and how to sort the message list. In the next lesson you will learn how to send a reply to a message.

REPLYING TO A MESSAGE

In this lesson you will learn how to send a response to a message and how to forward a message to other users.

ANSWERING A MESSAGE

Answering a message is easy. After you've read the message, you can quickly send a reply by using these steps:

1. Locate and read the message.

2. Click the Reply to Sender toolbar button, or press Ctrl+R. To send a reply to everyone listed in the To and Cc boxes, choose Reply to All or press Ctrl+Shift+R. Figure 7.1 illustrates the Reply dialog box.

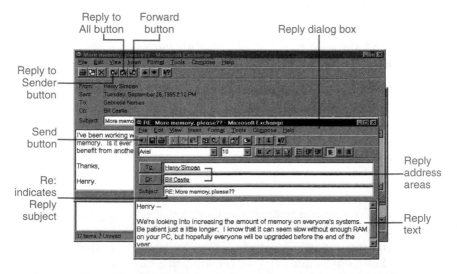

FIGURE 7.1 The Reply dialog box automatically completes the address areas.

3. You can add additional recipients to those listed in the To or Cc boxes. See Lesson 5 if you need to review how to address a message.

4. You can change the subject line to reflect your reply text.

5. Click inside the message area and type your reply. You can use any message formatting commands just as you normally would.

6. When your reply message is complete, click the Send button or press Ctrl+Enter. The message will go to your Outbox folder, then to your Sent Items folder.

INCLUDING THE ORIGINAL MESSAGE IN YOUR REPLY

It can be useful to include the original message text in your reply. This allows you to either annotate the text, or just add your own thoughts. Including the original text in a reply is the default action for Exchange. You can turn off the text inclusion, or turn it back on using the following steps:

1. Choose Tools, Options.

2. Click the Read tab. You will see the dialog box shown in Figure 7.2.

3. If not already checked, click the checkbox Include the original text when replying. You can click the checkbox again to remove the check mark. You can also choose to indent the original text in your reply, or to close the original item. Closing the original item removes the original message from your screen before you type your response.

4. If you want to change the font used for your reply, click the Font button to open the Font dialog box. The Font dialog box allows you to change the default font used when replying to a message. You can learn more about changing default fonts for replying to a message in Lesson 23. Click OK to return to the Options dialog box.

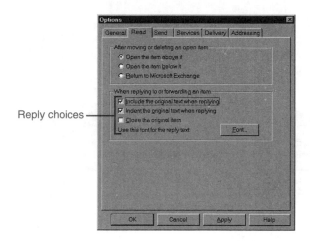

FIGURE 7.2   The Read tab of the Options dialog box allows you to set reply choices.

5. Click OK when your choices are complete.

6. Now follow the steps listed in the previous section for Answering a Message.

FORWARDING A MESSAGE

Forwarding a Message sends the original message to users other than the original sender. For example, if you want to write a message back to the original sender, you would send a *reply*. On the other hand, if you want to send the message to another person, you would *forward* the message. You can include a subject line and personal comments with the forwarded message. The following steps are used to forward a message.

1. Locate the message you want to forward. You can forward a message either while reading the message or from the folder list.

2. Click the Forward button, or press Ctrl+F. The Forward message dialog box will open, as shown in Figure 7.3.

Can't forward a fax? Be sure that you are not in the Fax viewer when you choose to forward a fax. Select the fax message in your Folder list, then choose Forward.

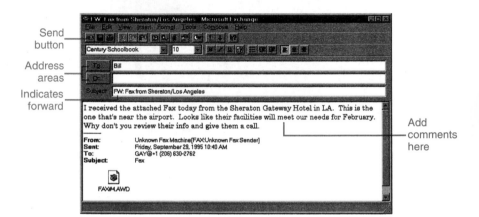

Send button

Address areas

Indicates forward

Add comments here

FIGURE 7.3   Forwarding a message.

3. Complete the To and Cc boxes as necessary.

4. The subject line will indicate that the message is being forwarded with an FW before the subject text. You can edit the subject line if you choose.

5. Click in the message area, then type any comments you want to include with the forwarded message.

6. Send the message by clicking the Send button or pressing Ctrl+Enter.

In this lesson you learned how to send a response to a message and how to forward a message to other users. In the next lesson you will learn how to print your messages.

PRINTING A MESSAGE

In this lesson you will learn how to print your messages.

You will generally maintain and organize your messages electronically using Exchange's folder system, but having a paper copy of a message can sometimes be useful. Printing a message allows you to give a copy to someone whose e-mail system is not compatible with Exchange; take a copy with you to a meeting; or just sit back, relax, and ponder the message.

PRINTING MESSAGES FROM THE EXCHANGE VIEWER

With Exchange, you can print a message in many different ways. You can use the Print dialog box, or you can print a message using a Toolbar button without setting any options. Both of these methods are illustrated in this lesson. You can print one message or several messages at the same time. You can even print a message from the Exchange Viewer message list without opening it first. The button method is a quick way to print selected messages, but the menu route allows you more flexibility in changing print options.

Sending a message to print, or any other file or document in any application, is often referred to as *submitting a print job*. Print jobs are usually *routed* (sent) to your default printer unless you choose an alternate printer when you submit the job. Of course, you must have more than one printer available before you can choose an alternate. A *default printer*, therefore, is the one you print to unless another printer is chosen.

You may be using a local printer (probably right there on your desk or work table), or you may be limited to using a network printer, which you'll share with others on the network. Either one may be your default printer.

Your default printer is usually determined at the time you install Windows 95. You can, however, change your default printer if needed by clicking the Start menu on your Windows 95 desktop. Then choose Settings, Printers. Select the printer you want to set as default, then right-click and select Set as default. Be aware that a default printer is the default for all programs you use in Windows 95. This means that when you send a print job in your word processing program, it will also be sent to your default printer unless you then choose an alternate printer using that program's print dialog box.

One last term you should be aware of before continuing with this lesson is *spool*. When you send a job to print, that job first writes to a temporary file. Then it spools directly to the printer or perhaps to some other print program on a network.

PRINTING USING THE PRINT BUTTON

You can quickly send one or several messages to your default printer by using the Print button on the toolbar. Use the steps which follow:

1. Select the folder which contains the message(s) you want to print. If your folder list is not visible, choose View, Folders, or click the Show/Hide Folder List button on the Toolbar.

2. Select the message or messages to be printed. As displayed in Figure 8.1, you can select messages that are listed together by clicking on the first message, then pressing Shift while clicking on the last message in the group. To select messages that are not listed together, press the Ctrl key while clicking on each message.

3. Click the Print button on the toolbar. The messages will spool to your default printer. A dialog box will briefly

appear on-screen telling you that the messages are being printed. You'll also see the name of the printer to which the messages are being sent displayed in the dialog box.

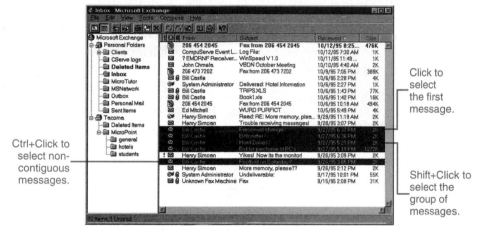

Click to select the first message.

Ctrl+Click to select non-contiguous messages.

Shift+Click to select the group of messages.

FIGURE 8.1 Select messages to be printed.

Messages all on the same page? When printing several selected messages using the Print button, each message will print one after the other on the same page. If you want each message to start on a separate sheet of paper, use the menu commands instead of using the Print button to print messages (see the following sections for instructions).

PRINTING USING THE MENU COMMANDS

Using the menus to print allows you to select an alternate printer, to direct Exchange to start printing each message on a separate page, to print any message attachments, and to print multiple copies of a message. If needed, you can also specify any necessary changes to your current printer properties.

Use the steps which follow to print from the Exchange Viewer menus:

1. Select the message(s) to be printed. You can select messages that are listed together by clicking on the first message, then pressing Shift while clicking on the last message in the group. To select messages that are not listed together, press the Ctrl key while clicking on each message.

2. Choose File, Print or press Ctrl+P. Alternatively, right-click to see the shortcut menu, then select Print. The Print dialog box will appear as displayed in Figure 8.2.

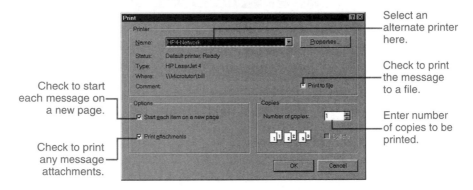

Select an alternate printer here.

Check to start each message on a new page.

Check to print the message to a file.

Check to print any message attachments.

Enter number of copies to be printed.

FIGURE 8.2   The Print dialog box allows you to customize your print job.

3. Click any print options you need. Choose the options from the list below:

   Name   The Name field is used to select the printer to which you want to send the current print job. Notice that the Status, Type, Where and Comment fields reflect information pertinent to the printer listed in the Name field. (You can't change the values in these fields—they are informational only.) You can either type the name of an alternate printer in the Name field, or click the list button to select an alternate printer.

Start each item on a new page   When printing several messages, you'll want to click this checkbox to be sure that each message starts on a separate page. If the box is unchecked, messages will print sequentially, one after the other on the same page. (Of course, as each page is full, a new page will be started.)

Print attachments   When printing a message with an attachment, be sure to click this checkbox so that the attachment will also print. If the box is not checked, any message text will print, but the attachment will not print (a small icon will print, instead).

Number of copies   If you need to print more than one copy of your message, change the number of copies to be printed by either typing the correct number or selecting a number using the *spin control* (the up & down buttons on the edge of the field). If you've chosen to print more than one copy, you can also check the collate field to sequentially print all pages of the message for each print cycle. If the collate field is not checked, the message will print each page the specified number of times before printing the next page. For example, if you've chosen to print 3 copies of the message, 3 page 1's will print, then 3 page 2's, then 3 page 3's, and so on when the collate field is not checked.

Print to file   Checking the Print to file option forces the message to be printed to a file rather than to a printer. You will be prompted to enter the name of the file to which you want the message printed.

4. When finished making your print selections, click OK.

PRINTING FROM THE MESSAGE VIEW

A message can be printed while it is open for reading using one of the following two methods:

1. Open the message by double-clicking on the message.

2. Click the Print button. The message text will print.

or

1. Open the message by double-clicking on the message.

2. Choose File, Print, or press Ctrl+P.

3. Complete the Print dialog box, then choose OK.

In this lesson you learned how to print a message. In the next lesson, you will learn how to add files, messages and objects as attachments to your mail messages. You will also learn how to open and read an attachment, how to print attachments, and how to save attachments as files on your system.

ADDING ATTACHMENTS TO YOUR MESSAGES

In this lesson you will learn how to add files, messages and objects as attachments to your mail messages. You will also learn how to open and read an attachment, how to print attachments and how to save attachments as files on your system.

An attachment is a file, object, or another message which is included in a message you send or receive. By including an attachment, you can quickly forward a complete file such as a document, spreadsheet, or graphic with the text of your message. You can also include a message you received as an attachment to a message you are sending. Alternatively, you can include an *object* with your message.

Object   An object is a piece of information which is created by another Windows application that has OLE (*ob*ject *l*inking and *e*mbedding) capabilities. Objects can be linked or embedded in other applications, such as Exchange. An *embedded* object is stored within the recipient application. When you double-click an object, the application used to create the object opens, allowing you to edit the object.

You can read an attachment if you have the same application that was used to create the attachment. For example, suppose you receive a message that contains a spreadsheet originally created in Microsoft Excel. You can only open and read the attached spreadsheet if you have Excel available to you. You'll receive an error message and won't be able to open and read an attachment if you don't have the application available.

ADDING AN ATTACHMENT TO A MESSAGE

You can add attachments to your message using either menu commands or the drag and drop techniques of Windows 95.

To add an attachment, use the following general steps. More information about each of the attachment types can be found in the sections which follow.

1. Compose your message. See Lesson 5 if you need to review the steps.

2. When you are ready to add the attachment, choose Insert. Then choose the attachment type you want to use— File, Message, or Object.

3. Complete the dialog box for the attachment type you have chosen, then choose OK. Depending on the attachment options you selected, you'll either see an icon in your message which indicates you have attached a file, or the complete text of the file you attached.

4. Repeat steps 1-3 for each attachment you want to include in your message.

USING A FILE AS A MESSAGE ATTACHMENT

Follow these steps to use a file as an attachment to your message:

1. Compose the text of your message.

2. Choose Insert, File. You will see the Insert File dialog box as displayed in Figure 9.1.

3. Locate the file you want to include in your message and click on the file name.

4. Choose between adding the file as text or as an actual attachment to the message. You can also choose to *link* the file.

5. Choose OK.

 Link   Linking a file connects that file to your message. The linked file is then actually connected with both the message and its host application. When you read a file linked to a message, you actually open both the application and the file—the actual file, not a *copy* of the file. If you have network rights to do so, you can even edit the linked file as you read it. When you choose to link, you may also be asked to type the complete path to the file.

 Drag attachment to message   It can be faster to drag an existing file into an open message box. To do so, open both the message you are composing and the list (such as My Computer or the Windows Explorer) which contains the file you want to include. Click and drag the file from the list into the message. The file will be added as an attachment to your message.

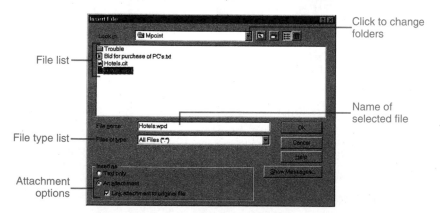

FIGURE 9.1   The Insert File dialog box appears when attaching a file to a message.

USING ANOTHER MESSAGE AS A MESSAGE ATTACHMENT

As you learned in Lesson 7, messages can easily be forwarded to another user. Just as easily, you can attach an existing message to another message. This can be useful when you want to include the message as one of several attachments. To attach a message, use these steps:

1. Compose the text of your message.

2. When you are ready to attach the message, choose Insert, Message. You will see the Insert Message dialog box as displayed in Figure 9.2.

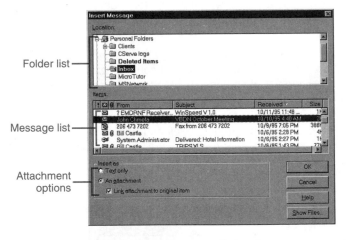

Folder list

Message list

Attachment options

FIGURE 9.2   The Insert Message dialog box appears when attaching a message to a message.

3. In the Location area, choose the folder which contains the message you want to attach.

4. In the Items area, choose the message you want to attach.

5. Choose any attachment options you want to use.

6. Choose OK.

USING AN OBJECT AS A MESSAGE ATTACHMENT

Existing objects can be attached to messages, or you can design or create the object in another application and then attach it to your message.

To use an object in a message:

1. Compose the message text.

2. When you are ready to attach the object, choose Insert, Object. The Insert Object dialog box will appear as shown in Figure 9.3.

For new objects, choose the object type here.

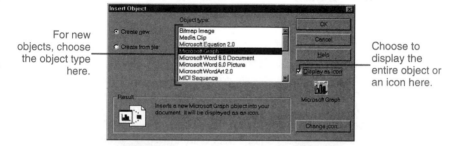

Choose to display the entire object or an icon here.

FIGURE 9.3 The Insert Object dialog box appears when attaching an object to a message.

3. You are given the option of creating a new object or using an existing object file. If you want to create a new object, click on the Create new option button. In the Object type list, choose the object type. The application used to create the object will open and allow you to create your object.

4. If you choose to use an existing object file, click on the Create from file option button. The Insert Object dialog box will change, as displayed in Figure 9.4.

5. In the Create from file box, type the name of the file you want to link or include in your message. Be sure to include the full path for the file. If you don't know the name of the file, or want to pick it from a list of files, click

the Browse button. The Browse dialog box will open. Select the file you want to use, then click Open. The file you
have chosen will appear in the Create from file box.

6. Click the Link button if you want to link the file with
   your message. (A file that is not linked will not be updated if changes are made to the file.)

7. Click the Display as icon button to display the object as
   an icon in the message. If you *do not* click the Display as
   icon button, the entire file will be embedded (copied) in
   your message. Note that if that file is also linked, only a
   "picture" of the file is embedded. That embedded picture
   will be updated if the original file is changed.

 Linked and unlinked icon objects? Both linked and
unlinked objects can appear as icons in a message. The
linked object will display the filename under the icon,
while an unlinked object will display the type of file represented by the icon (for example, "document" or "spreadsheet"). A linked object will contain the most current
changes in the object file. An unlinked object will display
the copy as it appeared when the message was written.

Click to
choose a
file from the
file list.

Click to link
the object
file to the
message.

Display
the object
as an icon
here.

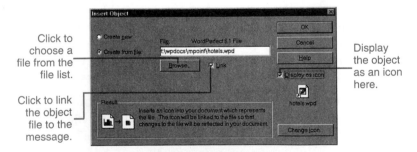

FIGURE 9.4   The Insert Object dialog box changes when attaching a file object.

8. Choose OK. You will be returned to the New Message
   dialog box.

Reading an Object Displayed as an Icon To read an object displayed as an icon in a message you receive, double-click the icon. The associated application will open and display the object.

OPENING AND READING MESSAGE ATTACHMENTS

Messages which contain attachments are displayed with a paperclip in your Inbox. A fully contained (embedded) attachment can be read within the message as standard message text. Attachments that appear as icons within the message must be opened before you can view and edit its contents. To open an attachment:

1. Select the message which contains the attachment from your message list.

2. Press Enter, or double-click on the message.

3. Double-click the icon which represents the attachment. If you have the software associated with the attachment, the attachment will open and you can read and edit its contents. Figure 9.5 illustrates a message with an open attachment.

File doesn't exist! A file attachment which is linked across a network may cause the error message "does not exist." The file very well may exist; however, Exchange doesn't always perform the link properly. The only work-around is to not link files across a network. A link will also fail if the recipient of your message does not have permission to open a file or if your message was sent using the Internet or an online service.

Associated application starts and opens attachment.

Paperclip indicates attachment to message.

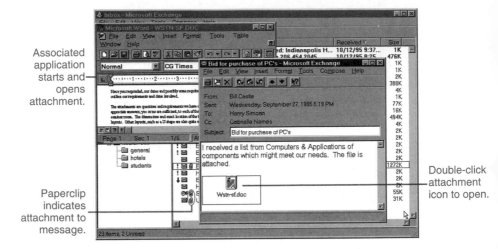

Double-click attachment icon to open.

FIGURE 9.5   Opened attachments can be edited.

PRINTING MESSAGES THAT CONTAIN ATTACHMENTS

A simple method to print attachments is:

1. From the message list (such as your Inbox), highlight the message or messages you want to print.

2. Choose File, Print, or press Ctrl+P.

3. Click the check box Print attachments, then choose OK. Exchange will open the associated application, open the attachment and then print the attachment from that application. When the print job is finished, Exchange will close the attachment and application.

You can also print an attachment while reading it. Using this method, you print using the normal print steps for that application. For example, if you are reading an attachment that is associated with Microsoft Word, use the steps in Word to print the attachment.

SAVING AN ATTACHMENT AS A FILE

If you want to save an attachment received in a message as an individual file, you can use one of the following methods:

- Open the attachment, then use the File Save or File Save As commands within the associated application.

- Open the message, click the attachment icon, then choose File, Save As. You will see the dialog box displayed in Figure 9.6. Select the drive and folder you want to use to save the message and then type the name of the file in the Filename text box if necessary. Make certain that the attachment(s) you want saved are selected in the Save these attachments box, make sure the Save these Attachments only option button is selected, then click on Save.

- Open the message, click the attachment icon, then right-click to get the shortcut menu. Click Save As. You will see the dialog box displayed in Figure 9.6. Select the drive and folder to which you want to save the message. Type the name of the file in the Filename text box, if necessary, then click Save.

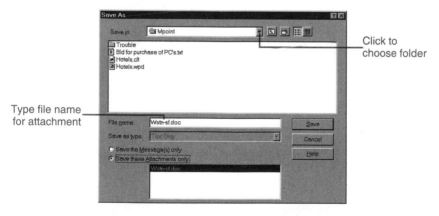

FIGURE 9.6   The Save As dialog box allows you to save message attachments.

- Open either My Computer or Explorer from Windows, select and display the folder in which you want to store the attachment. Next, open the message and click the attachment icon. Now drag the attachment icon to the folder displayed in My Computer. The attachment will be saved to the folder using its original filename. An unnamed object is saved as a Scrap object.

In this lesson, you learned how to add files, messages and objects as attachments to your mail messages. You also learned how to open, read, and print attachments and save them as files on your system. In the next lesson, you will learn how to organize your messages by creating personal folders and how to move messages to your personal folders.

MANAGING YOUR MESSAGES

In this lesson you will learn how to organize your messages by creating personal folders. You will also learn how to delete and undelete messages and how to empty the Deleted Items folder.

In a very short time, your Inbox will contain a profusion of messages. You'll have messages you no longer need that should be deleted. Other messages, however, need to be kept or stored. You may want to logically organize messages regarding similar matters. For example, you may have messages from clients, messages from co-workers regarding personal matters, messages regarding corporate policies, and so on. Allowing messages to pile up in the Inbox will result in chaos.

Four folders exist when Exchange is started: Inbox, Outbox, Deleted Items and Sent Items. When the folder list is displayed, these four folders will be displayed under the Personal Folders folder icon. These folders are automatically created and cannot be deleted or renamed. But, you can create additional personal folders and subfolders to organize your messages in a logical order.

Personal folders are similar to any other folder organization scheme within Windows 95. For example, you might wish to create a set of folders for each department in your firm. Therefore, a folder might be created for the Sales department, one for Accounting, one for Personnel, and another for Engineering. Within each of these folders, you can also create subfolders. So within the Personnel folder, you might create subfolders for New Employees, Employee Reviews, Employee Benefits, and so on.

In addition to storing and organizing messages in folders, you can also store files or other objects in Exchange folders. You could, therefore, drag a spreadsheet file into the Accounting folder. This allows you to keep supporting files all together in one location.

The Folder view must be visible prior to adding new folders. Remember that the Folder view only appears if you have selected it from the View menu, or started Exchange for the first time from the Start, Programs menu of Windows 95. If your folder list is not visible, choose View, Folders, or click the Show/Hide Folder List button on the Toolbar.

You can create as many personal folders as you need. You can then create subfolders under the personal folders, sub-subfolders, and so on. All personal folder sets used within Exchange reside under the Microsoft Exchange icon. To expand a list of folders, click the plus (+) icon to the left of the folder icon. The folder set will open, displaying all subfolders which reside beneath it. See Figure 10.1. Similarly, click the minus (-) icon to condense the list.

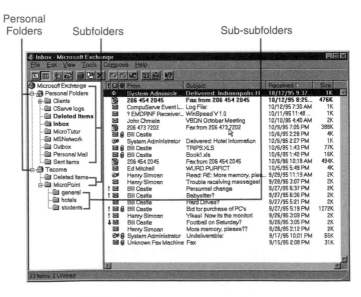

FIGURE 10.1   Folders allow you to organize your messages.

CREATING A NEW PERSONAL FOLDER SERVICE

All messaging components of Exchange are considered to be *services*. Three services are automatically included when Exchange is installed—Microsoft Mail service, Personal Folders service, and the Personal Address Book service. Other services can be added such as Microsoft Fax services, CompuServe mail services, Internet mail services, and additional Personal Folder services.

A new Personal Folder service automatically contains a subfolder named Deleted Items (you'll learn more about this folder in the following sections in this lesson). To create a new Personal Folders service:

1. From the Exchange Viewer, choose Tools, Services. Then click the Add button.

2. Click Personal Folders, then choose OK.

3. Choose the Windows 95 location where your personal folders are stored. (Exchange usually places them in the Exchange folder.) Then type the name for your new personal folder file in the File name field. Exchange will automatically add a .PST extension when it creates the personal folder file.

4. Choose Open. The Create Personal Folders dialog box will appear as shown in Figure 10.2.

FIGURE 10.2   The Create Personal Folders dialog box is used to add a new Personal Folders service to Exchange.

5. In the Name field, type the descriptive name you want to use for the Personal Folders service. (The descriptive name appears in the Exchange folder list display.)

6. Even if password-protected, any text in a personal folder file can be opened by other programs as a text file unless you have chosen some type of encryption. An encrypted file appears as gibberish to other programs. If you want to include encryption for your new personal folder service, click the option you want to use. A brief description of each option is listed below:

    No Encryption Clicking No Encryption allows the contents of the personal folder files to be read by other programs.

    Compressible Encryption Compressible Encryption provides a moderate form of file encryption so that it cannot be read by most other programs. The format used also allows the personal folder files to be compressed so that they take up less space on your hard disk.

    Best Encryption This option provides the best degree of protection against the file being read by another program. Personal folder files which use Best Encryption cannot be compressed, however.

7. You can also optionally add a password to a personal folders service. If you have assigned a password to your personal folder sevice, you will be prompted to enter the password each time you start Exchange or use the personal folders. To do so, type a password in the Password field, then re-type it in the Verify Password field. This assures that you have not made an error while typing your password.

    If you want to, you can also save the password in your password list. However, in doing so you are allowing anyone who uses your system and shares your profile access to your personal folder. If checked, you will only be asked for a password if you have logged on to Exchange using a different name.

8. Choose OK to return to the Services dialog box, then OK again to return to the Exchange Viewer. The new personal folder service will appear in your folder list.

CREATING NEW SUBFOLDERS

You can create a subfolder to any existing folder whenever necessary. To do so, use the following steps:

1. Be sure the Folder view is visible.

2. Click the personal folders icon under which you want the new subfolder to appear.

3. Choose File, New Folder.

4. Type the name you want to use for the new folder in the Folder name field, then choose OK. The new folder will appear in your folder list.

To create a sub-subfolder:

1. Be sure the Folder view is visible.

2. Click the subfolder under which you want to create a sub-subfolder.

3. Choose File, New Folder.

4. Type the name you want to use for the new sub-subfolder in the Folder name field, then choose OK.

5. The new sub-subfolder will appear beneath its parent subfolder.

TIP **To View/Hide Subfolders**   To open or close a folder hierarchy, click the plus (+) symbol to expand the folder list or the minus (-) symbol to condense the folder list. See Figure 10.3.

All folders reside beneath the Microsoft Exchange icon.   Parent folders are preceded by a [+] or [-].

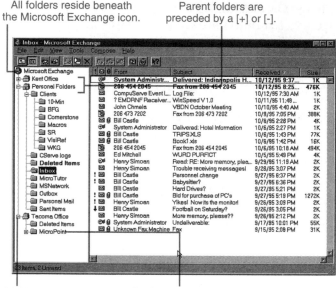

All subfolders are displayed for this parent folder.   Subfolders exist which are not displayed.

FIGURE 10.3   Personal folders are used to logically organize messages.

MOVING MESSAGES AND FILES TO A FOLDER

Once you have created the folder heirarchy you want to use, it is easy to move messages to a folder. Use these steps:

1. Be sure the Folder view is visible.

2. Click the folder icon to open the contents of the folder. For example, click the Inbox icon to view the contents of your Inbox.

3. Select the message or messages you want to move to the folder.

4. Drag the selected messages to your desired folder icon. The messages will be moved to the new folder.

 TIP   **Copying Messages**   You can also copy a message by holding the Ctrl key while dragging the message to a folder. This leaves the message in its original folder location while duplicating it in another folder.

DELETING AND "UNDELETING" MESSAGES

Messages files are often very large files. Some messages might contain the entire text from a long document file, or perhaps a several-page fax message has been delivered to your Inbox. These files can accumulate rapidly, wasting valuable disk space. You should get in the habit, therefore, of regularly cleaning house— deleting messages which are no longer needed.

To delete messages:

1. Display the folder which contains the messages to be deleted.

2. Select the message or messages to be deleted.

3. Press the Delete key. The messages will be deleted from the current folder and sent to the Deleted Items folder.

The Deleted Items folder will help you gracefully recover from messages which were deleted in error. All messages, or files, which are deleted from a personal folder are automatically stored in the Deleted Items folder.

To undelete a message, follow these steps:

1. Display the contents of the Deleted Items folder.

2. Locate and select the message or messages to be undeleted.

3. Copy or move the selected messages to the folder to which you want them restored.

EMPTYING THE DELETED ITEMS FOLDER

Deleting messages from personal folders *doesn't* delete them from your hard disk. Deleted messages are sent to the Deleted Items folder. When you then delete the messages from the Deleted Items folder, they are deleted from the hard disk.

Think of the Deleted Items folder as the trash basket in which you throw papers for a week. If necessary, you can easily (although not necessarily happily), riffle through the trash basket to find a paper thrown away by mistake. The trash basket continues to accumulate trash until emptied.

Similarly, the Deleted Items folder accumulates deleted messages until emptied. To *empty the trash*, use these steps:

1. Display the contents of the Deleted Items folder.

2. Select the messages to be permanently deleted.

3. Press the **Delete** key or click the **Delete** button on the Toolbar. Exchange will display a confirming warning message.

4. You should visually verify that you *do* want to permanently remove all selected messages from the system. The selected messages appear underlined when chosen for deletion. Drag the warning box out of the way so that you can more easily view the selected message list.

5. When you are satisfied that you do want to delete the messages, choose Yes. The messages will be deleted from your system.

In this lesson you learned how to organize your messages by creating personal folders, in addition to learning how to move and delete messages from your personal folders. In the next lesson you will learn how to open the address books and how to use Address Book entries in your messages.

USING THE EXCHANGE ADDRESS BOOKS

In this lesson you will learn how to open the address books and how to use Address Book entries in your messages.

This lesson differs slightly from other lessons in this book. You will learn what address books are and how they are used in Exchange. In addition, you will learn *how* to use existing address book entries in your messages. Lesson 12 will cover how to actually create entries in your address book.

THE PURPOSE OF ADDRESS BOOKS

Exchange automatically sets up two address books for you: a Personal Address Book and a Postoffice Address List. These two address books are an electronic method of storing the addresses of those users with whom you correspond. Addresses can be telephone numbers used for faxing, Internet Mail addresses, Microsoft Network addresses, CompuServe addresses, America Online addresses, or simply e-mail addresses for other users on your network. You can include complete location information for each of the entries you store in the address book, including multiple telephone numbers, pager numbers, and fax numbers. If you include telephone numbers in your address listings, you can also dial the number from the address book.

The Postoffice Address List contains the e-mail addresses of all persons who reside in your postoffice. If you are using Exchange on a stand-alone computer, then you are the only entry in the postoffice. On a network, the Postoffice Address List is usually stored on the network server. On a stand-alone system, both address books are kept on your own hard drive.

If you work on a network it can be useful to download the contents of the Postoffice Address List onto your own hard drive so that you can compose messages even when you are not connected to the network. (More information about working with Remote Mail can be found in Lesson 18.) Changes made to the Postoffice Address List on the network are not automatically made to the copy stored on your own hard drive. You'll need to download the Postoffice Address list periodically to keep it current. To download the Postoffice Address list, follow these steps:

1. From the Exchange Viewer, choose Tools, Microsoft Mail Tools.

2. Choose Download Address Lists. A dialog box will briefly appear as the address list is copied (downloaded). When the copy is complete, you will be returned to the Exchange Viewer.

The Personal Address Book contains entries which you have added for personal use and convenience. It can also contain entries which you have copied from another address book list into your Personal Address Book. You'll learn how to copy entries to your Personal Address Book in the next lesson. The Personal Address Book is typically kept on your own hard drive. Address books will also be created for each of the other online information services you use. For example, a new address book will be created if you subscribe to The Microsoft Network, which contains addresses for other Microsoft Network members.

OPENING AND UNDERSTANDING THE ADDRESS BOOK WINDOW

The easiest method to open your Address Book from the Exchange Viewer is to click the Address Book toolbar button. You can alternatively choose Tools, Address Book, or press Ctrl+Shift+B. Figure 11.1 displays a typical address book list.

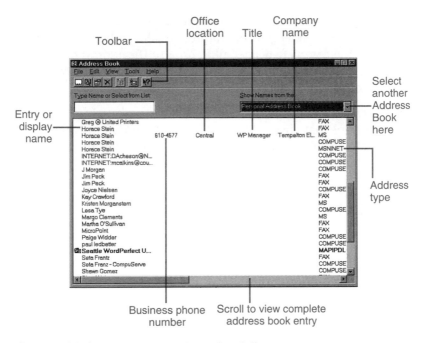

FIGURE 11.1   A sample address book list.

When you open an address book you'll see a list of all entries for that book. The list contains several fields for each entry, although you can't see all of the fields at the same time. All fields for an entry are referred to as *properties*. For example, an entry can include a display name (the name by which you identify the entry), US Mail information such as a street address, city, state and zip code, and several phone numbers.

There will also be a field compiled by the address book, which represents the complete address for the entry, based on the address type. You can easily view the properties for an entry by double-clicking the entry. You can alternatively select the entry, then click the Properties button in the Toolbar. Or, you can select an entry, then right-click to open the shortcut menu. Choose Properties. The Properties dialog box will appear for your selected entry. When you are finished, click OK to return to the Address Book window.

Several of the fields are displayed in the address book list. Think of these as the header information for an address book entry. You can't see the complete header all at once in the address book window—you'll need to use the horizontal scroll bar at the bottom of the window to view additional header fields.

Like most windows, the Address Book window contains a toolbar with buttons that are used to quickly access commonly used features. Rest the mouse pointer briefly on each button to view its tooltip. Table 11.1 lists the purpose of each button.

Table 11.1   Address Book toolbar buttons

Button	Name	Purpose
	New Entry	Allows you to add new address entries to your address book.
	Find	Allows you to find address entries in the currently displayed address book.
	Properties	Opens a dialog box for a selected address entry which can be used to store additional information for the entry.
	Delete	Permanently removes an entry from the address book.
	Add to Personal Address Book	Copies an entry from another address book to your Personal Address Book.
	New Message	Opens the New Message dialog box. The currently selected address entry will appear in the To: field.

BUTTON	NAME	PURPOSE
	Help	Changes the mouse pointer to the Help, Select pointer. You can then point and click on any window area to open its related help topic.

Close the Address Book by choosing File, Close, or pressing Alt+F4. You can also click the Windows Close button.

UNDERSTANDING ADDRESS TYPES

Exchange can be used as a vehicle to send e-mail to a variety of *MAPI* messaging services. Each of these information services use different addressing conventions, requiring a basic understanding of how address entries look. The next sections will fill you in on the appearance and technicalities of adding telephone numbers, fax numbers, Microsoft Mail addresses and addresses for online services.

> **MAPI** A Messaging Application Program Interface is a set of programming commands which allows other programs to send or receive mail.

TELEPHONE NUMBERS

Starting from the simplest address type, telephone numbers and street addresses can be stored as entries in your Personal Address Book. Telephone numbers can include country codes, city codes, area codes, and finally personal numbers. For example, if you correspond with Yangzhou, China, you might have a telephone number entry in your address book which reads: 011-86-514-234555. On the other hand, your telephone number entries might be as simple as its prefix and four-digit number: 555-1234. As displayed in Figure 11.2, each address book entry can contain a complete suite of telephone numbers, including several business numbers, personal numbers, pager numbers, and so on.

If you have a modem installed in Windows 95, you can automatically dial any of the telephone numbers stored in an address book entry, except for Fax numbers. Lesson 12 will help you add specific address book entries, including phone numbers. When phone numbers are stored with an address book entry, use the following steps to dial the telephone number:

1. From the Exchange Viewer, click the Address Book toolbar button. The Address Book list will appear.

2. If necessary, change address books by clicking the Show Names from the drop-down list button. Then select the name which contains the phone number you want to dial.

3. Right-click, then select Properties from the shortcut menu. The Properties dialog box will appear for the selected address book entry.

4. Click the Phone Number tab.

5. Click the Dial button beside the phone number to be dialed. Your modem will dial the number. When dialing is complete, pick up the handset on your telephone to finish your call.

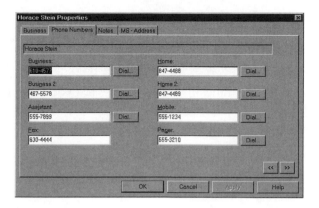

FIGURE 11.2   An address book entry stores a complete suite of telephone numbers.

FAX NUMBERS

As you know, you can use Exchange as a fax information service, both sending and receiving faxes using your fax modem. While fax numbers are usually thought of as *telephone numbers*, fax addresses used by Exchange Fax Services are entered as a separate entry in the address book. Fax numbers cannot be directly dialed from the address book entry. A sample fax entry can be seen in Figure 11.3.

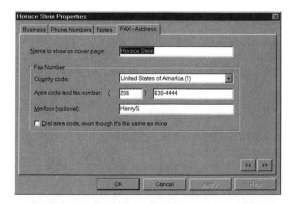

FIGURE 11.3   Fax entries have a unique address type in Exchange.

Microsoft Mail Addresses

Users in your postoffice receive their e-mail addresses as Microsoft Mail addresses. Exchange is limited to sending e-mail to users within your own Postoffice. If you also use Microsoft Exchange Server, or if you have added the Microsoft Mail Postoffice Upgrade, you can access addresses from multiple postoffices. A sample Microsoft Mail address entry can be seen in Figure 11.4.

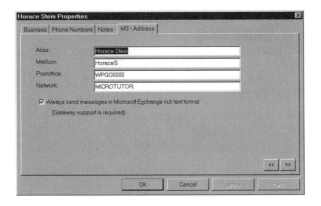

Figure 11.4 Microsoft Mail addresses are limited to one Postoffice in Exchange.

Addresses for Online Services

You can also store addresses for the various online services you use. If you send Internet mail using the Microsoft Network, for example, your address entries might look like Figure 11.5. A sample address entry for CompuServe is displayed in Figure 11.6.

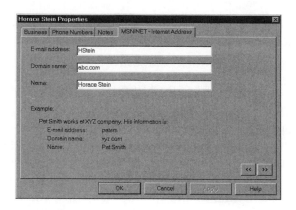

Figure 11.5 Internet addresses include an E-mail address and Domain name.

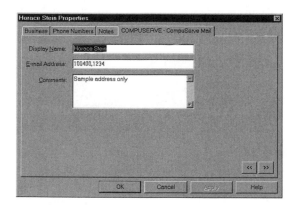

Figure 11.6 CompuServe addresses include a Display Name and E-Mail address.

Using Address Book Entries in Exchange Messages

Using address book entries in messages is simpler and more accurate than attempting to remember all of the user addresses to which you regularly send e-mail or faxes.

USING ADDRESS ENTRIES WHILE COMPOSING A MESSAGE

To use address entries when composing a message:

1. While in Exchange, choose Compose, New Message, or press Ctrl+N. The New Message dialog box will appear.

2. Click the Address Book button on the toolbar, or click any of the To, Cc, or Bcc (if displayed) buttons. The Address Book dialog box will appear (see Figure 11.7). The Address Book dialog box differs slightly from the full-blown Address Book window and appears only when you click an address button when composing a message. The Address Book dialog box contains a narrow list of address book entries. Similar to the Address Book window, you can select an alternate address book list from the Show Names from the drop-down list.

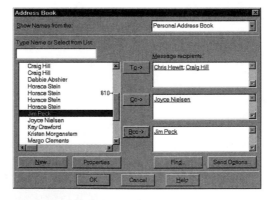

FIGURE 11.7 The Address Book window when opened from the Exchange Viewer.

3. In the Type Name or Select from List text box above the list, start typing a recipient's name. The cursor will move to the first name on the address list which matches your typed name. Alternatively, you can scroll through the list of available names, then click on the name to be used.

You can also select several names by holding down the
Shift or Ctrl keys while you click.

I can't find the name in the address list! If the name
you are seeking does not readily appear in the address
book list, use the Find function to search the current address book. Click the Find button on the Address Book
dialog box. The General dialog box will appear. Type a
portion of the name you want to find in the Find names
containing field and click OK to perform the search. Exchange will search the currently displayed address book
for the name you specified and will list all matches in a
resulting search list.

4. Click the To, Cc, or Bcc button to add the selected name
   to the Message recipients list.

5. Repeat steps 3 and 4 to add more names if desired.

6. When you finish adding names to the Message recipients
   list, choose OK. You will be returned to the New Message
   dialog box and the names will appear in their correct
   locations.

Duplicate Names! Exchange requires separate entries
for each address type. For example, you might have three
separate listings for John Smith: a fax listing, an MS Mail
listing, and a Microsoft Network listing. If you see duplicate names in your list, be sure to scroll the list to the right
or left so that you can view the listing type before you
select an entry.

CREATING A MESSAGE WHILE VIEWING AN ADDRESS BOOK

You can also compose a new message while you are viewing an address book. Use these steps:

1. From the Exchange Viewer, click the Address Book toolbar button, or choose Tools, Address Book, or press Ctrl+Shift+B. The Address Book window will open.

2. Select the name or names to whom you are addressing your message, then choose File, New Message, or press Ctrl+N. The New Message dialog box will appear with the names you have selected displayed in the To location.

3. Complete the message as you normally would, then send the message. You will be returned to the Address Book window.

In this lesson you have learned how to open the address books and how to use entries from an address book in your messages. In the next lesson you will learn how to add entries to your address books and how to create personal distribution lists.

ADDING ENTRIES TO THE ADDRESS BOOKS

In this lesson, you will learn how to add entries to your address books and how to create personal distribution lists.

Unless you are the administrator for your Microsoft Mail system, you should only add entries to your Personal Address Book. Each address type you add to your address book requires a slightly different set of instructions, depending on the complexity of the address.

Adding entries to the address books can be done either directly from the address book, or as you use the information service for which you need the address entry. For example, you can easily add a new fax entry to your address book as you prepare the fax.

As you can see in Figure 12.1, an address book listing can contain address types for many different services.

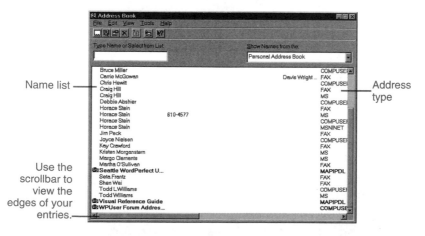

Name list —

Address type

Use the scrollbar to view the edges of your entries.

FIGURE 12.1 A Personal Address Book can contain entries for many services.

ADDING ENTRIES USING THE ADDRESS BOOK MENUS

Use the Address Book menus to quickly add entries for different address types. Each address type requires slightly different instructions for its particular addresses, however, the basic instructions are the same:

1. From the Exchange Viewer, choose the Address Book toolbar button, or choose Tools, Address Book (or press Ctrl+Shift+B). The Address Book dialog box will appear.

2. Click the New Entry toolbar button, or choose File, New Entry. The New Entry dialog box will appear as displayed in Figure 12.2. The address entry types will vary from those shown in Figure 12.2 since you may have different information services installed.

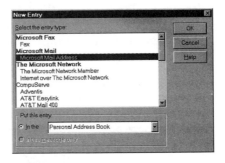

FIGURE 12.2   The New Entry dialog box is used to create entries for all of your information services.

3. Select Personal Address Book from the drop-down list under the Put this entry area.

4. Select the entry type you need from the Select the entry type list. See Lesson 11 for a description of the different types of entries.

5. Choose OK. The Address Properties dialog box which applies to your chosen address type will appear.

6. Complete the Address Properties dialog box. You'll need to supply the appropriate field information for each address type. You can use Exchange to send messages to many, many different addresses by using a combination of Microsoft Mail, Microsoft Fax, and a variety of online services. The syntax used for addresses for each of these information services are different. The next several sections of this lesson will help you complete the address requirements for Microsoft Mail, Microsoft Fax and The Microsoft Network. You'll need to know other specific information when sending e-mail using other online services.

7. Click OK when your address entry is complete. You will be returned to the Address Book dialog box.

 TIP **Other Address Information**   You can also store related address information and notes with an entry by clicking the Business, Phone Numbers, or Notes tab in the Address Properties dialog box.

8. Repeat steps 2 through 6 for each new address entry. When all entries are complete, click OK to close the New Properties dialog box. Then choose File, Close to return to the Exchange Viewer.

ADDING ENTRIES WHILE COMPOSING MESSAGES

All Exchange information services allow you to use Address Book entries as you create your messages. In general, the same steps are used to add address book entries for each message type:

1. Follow the steps to begin preparing your new message.

2. Click the button associated with the address area of your message. For example, click the To button when creating

a Mail message, or the Address Book button when creating a fax. The Address Book dialog box will appear as displayed in Figure 12.3.

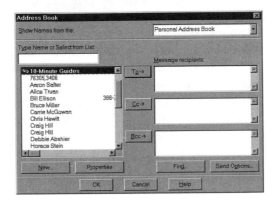

FIGURE 12.3   This Address Book dialog box appears when using the address book to address a message.

3. Click the New button. The New Entry dialog box will appear as shown in Figure 12.4.

Address types—

Address book to store the entry—

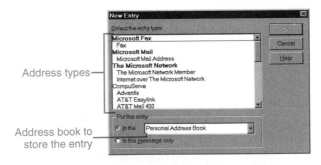

FIGURE 12.4   Select an entry type and address book to store your new entry.

4. Select the appropriate address type from the list.

5. Select the Personal Address Book from the Put this entry In the drop-down list.

6. Choose OK.

7. Complete the Properties dialog box for the address type, then choose OK. You will be returned to the dialog box where you can continue to compose your message.

ADDING MICROSOFT MAIL ENTRIES

Microsoft Mail entries are used to send messages to other users on your network who reside within your postoffice. If you are working on a stand-alone system (not on a network), you can skip this section. In the Windows 95 version of Exchange, you can only access Microsoft Mail entries for the postoffice to which you are attached. If you use Exchange Server or have added the Microsoft Mail Post Office Upgrade, you can send mail to other postoffices as well.

ADDING NEW ENTRIES

When adding a Microsoft Mail user to your Personal Address Book, you must know their mailbox, postoffice, and network name. Be sure to check with your Microsoft Mail administrator if you do not know each of these important elements.

You can add entries to your Personal Address Book by creating new entries directly through the Address Book. Just follow these steps:

1. Follow the steps 1 through 3 listed in a previous section called "Adding Entries Using the Address Book Menus."

2. Select the Microsoft Mail Address type from the entry type list, then click OK.

3. Click in the Alias text box, then type the *alias* to be used for this entry.

Alias   Often referred to as a "display name," an alias is the name you will use when you address a message to this user. The alias can be the user's complete name, a combination of initials and name, or an unrelated descriptive word or phrase, such as a pen name or nickname.

4. Click in the Mailbox text box, then type the name of this user's mailbox. The mailbox name is assigned to the user by the Mail administrator.

5. Click in the Postoffice text box, then type the name of the postoffice.

6. Click in the Network text box, then type the name of the network used for this address.

Address Book entry doesn't deliver the mail!
Although you can add entries to your Personal Address Book for postoffices other than your own, the Windows 95 Exchange does not support mail delivery to multiple postoffices. You can only send mail to postoffices other than your own if you are using Exchange Server or the Microsoft Mail Server.

7. If appropriate, click the checkbox for Rich text format.

Rich Text Format   Messages which use rich text format (RTF) include formatting such as underlining, boldface type, and different typefaces. While most Microsoft-compatible applications can read messages in rich text format, many online services cannot. Review formatting messages in Lesson 5 for more information regarding RTF.

8. When you are satisfied with the entry, choose OK.

COPYING ENTRIES FROM THE POSTOFFICE ADDRESS LIST

The easiest method of adding Microsoft Mail entries to your Personal Address book is to copy them from the Postoffice list. Use these steps:

1. Click the Address Book toolbar button.

2. Select the Postoffice Address List from the Show Names drop-down list.

3. Select those names to be copied to your Personal Address Book.

4. Choose File, Add to Personal Address Book.

5. Verify that the copy was successful by displaying the Personal Address Book from the Show Names drop-down list.

Other address lists will automatically be created as you add new information services. For example, if you add CompuServe as an information service, an address list named CompuServe Address Book will be created. You can copy address entries from those lists to your Personal Address Book in a similar fashion.

ADDING FAX ENTRIES

Fax entries are used to send faxes with your fax modem. To add a fax entry to your Personal Address Book, follow these steps:

1. Follow the steps 1 through 3 listed in a previous section called "Adding Entries Using the Address Book Menus."

2. Choose the Fax address type from the entry type list, then choose OK. The New Fax Properties dialog box shown in Figure 12.5 will appear.

3. Click in the Name to show on cover page: text box, then type the name to be used with the address entry.

4. Choose the country code to be used with the entry from the drop-down list. This code is used when dialing a long

distance fax call. A country code is typically used when placing a long distance call, although you may choose not to include it if you use some type of proprietary dialing sequence. For example, if you select the USA, a 1 will be dialed before any long distance call. If you choose Aruba, on the other hand, 297 will be dialed prior to the remaining digits. If you do not want a country code included with the entry, select (None-Dial as Entered) from the Country code drop-down list.

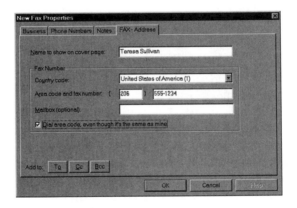

FIGURE 12.5   The New Fax Properties dialog box lets you create fax address entries.

5. Click in the area code and fax number text boxes, typing the correct numbers for each.

6. If this fax recipient also has a mailbox in your mail system, list their postoffice name in the Mailbox text box.

7. Click the checkbox for Dial area code, even though it's the same as mine if the area code for the fax entry matches yours and you want Fax services to dial the area code when a fax is sent. This is useful when the fax number prefix is a long distance call for you.

8. If you are adding a new address while creating a message, you can now use your new entry in your message by

clicking the To, Cc or Bcc buttons which appear at the bottom of the New Fax Properties dialog box.

9. When your entry is complete, choose OK.

CREATING PERSONAL DISTRIBUTION LISTS

A personal distribution list is used to group address entries so that messages can quickly be addressed to everyone in the list. You might want to create distribution lists for all members of a department, club, or project. To use a personal distribution list in your messages, select it from the address book list just as you would any other address book entry.

To create a personal distribution list:

1. Follow steps 1 through 3 in a previous section called Adding Entries Using the Address Book Menus.

2. From the New Entry dialog box, choose Personal Distribution List as the address type. A partially completed distribution list is shown in Figure 12.6.

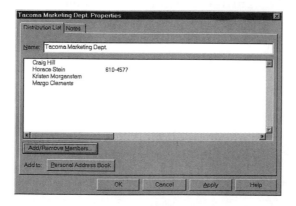

FIGURE 12.6   The New Personal Distribution List Properties dialog box with a completed entry.

3. Click in the Name text box, then type the name you want to use for this distribution list.

4. Click on the Add/Remove Members button. The address book list dialog box will appear.

5. Select those addresses you want to include in the Personal Distribution List. You can choose addresses from any of your address books and combine them in a single Personal Distribution List. Click Members to add the addresses to the list.

6. When you have selected all addresses, click OK. You will be returned to the New Personal Distribution List Properties dialog box and all of the addresses you selected will appear in your new personal distribution list.

7. Click OK to return to the Address Book list. Your new Personal Distribution List will appear in the list.

8. Choose File, Close to return to the Exchange Viewer.

In this lesson you learned how to add entries to your address books and how to create personal distribution lists. In the next lesson you will learn how to make changes to existing address entries and how to delete address entries you no longer need.

Maintaining Address Book Entries

*In this lesson you will learn how to
make changes to existing address entries and how to delete
address entries you no longer need.*

It's a fact of life that nothing ever stays the same for long. The
same can be said for your address book entries. At some point you
will need to make changes to the entries in your Personal Address
book. And, in the manner of good housekeeping, you should also
delete those entries you no longer need or which are invalid.

Modifying Existing Address Book Entries

All of the information stored with an address book entry is considered that entry's *properties*. Therefore, to make a change to an
address book entry, you modify the properties for the entry. You
can't change the address type, only the values for the defined
address can be changed. If you need to reassign an address type
for an entry, you must delete the entry, then recreate it for the
new address type. The steps for deleting an entry appear later in
this lesson.

Use the following steps to modify an address entry:

1. From the Exchange Viewer, click the Address Book
   toolbar button, or select Tools, Address Book.

2. You can access the Properties dialog using one of several
   methods:

- Select the entry to be changed, then click the Properties toolbar button.

- Select the entry to be changed, then choose File, Properties.

- Select the entry to be changed, then right-click. The shortcut menu will appear. Choose Properties.

- Double-click an entry.

The Properties dialog box will appear for the entry you have chosen. It will be specific to the address type assigned to the entry and will list all of its associated property elements. A sample Properties dialog box is shown in Figure 13.1.

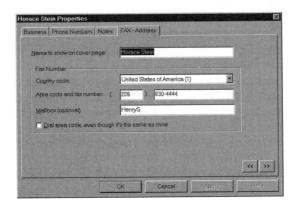

FIGURE 13.1   The Properties dialog box differs depending on the address type associated with the entry.

3. Make any necessary changes to the displayed dialog box. You can access associated address information by clicking any of the tabs at the top of the dialog box.

4. When you are satisfied with all of your changes, choose OK. You will be returned to the Address Book list.

MODIFYING PERSONAL DISTRIBUTION LISTS

You can also easily change a Personal Distribution List that you have already defined. You might wish to add additional members, or even remove some members from the list. Use these steps:

1. From the Exchange Viewer, click the Address Book Toolbar button, or select Tools, Address Book.

2. Select the Personal Distribution List from the address book entries, then double-click to quickly open its associated Properties dialog box. (You can alternatively use any of the previously discussed methods of accessing the Properties dialog box.)

3. Click the Add/Remove Members button. The Edit Members of... dialog box will open which is specific to the Personal Distribution List you selected.

4. To add new members, select their names from the address entry list, then click the Members button. The selected name(s) will be added to the member list.

5. To delete members, click the member name in the Personal Distribution List column, then press the Delete button. The member will be removed from the Personal Distribution List column, but will not be deleted from the address book.

6. When you have completed your changes, click OK to return to the Properties dialog box, then click OK to return to the Address Book. Choose File, Close to return to the Exchange Viewer.

DELETING ADDRESS BOOK ENTRIES

To help keep your Address Book organized, you should delete those addresses you no longer use. Unlike adding entries, you can only delete entries from the Address Book menus, you cannot delete entries while creating a new message.

To delete address book entries, use the following steps:

1. Open the Address Book from the Exchange Viewer.

2. Select the entries to be deleted.

3. Press the Delete key or click the Delete button from the toolbar. Alternatively, you can right-click to access the shortcut menu. Then choose Delete. As displayed in Figure 13.2, Exchange will ask you to confirm that you want to delete the selected entries.

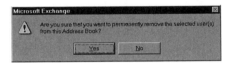

FIGURE 13.2   Confirm that you want to delete address book entries.

4. If you are confident that you no longer need the selected entries, choose Yes. If you are not sure, choose No. If you accidentally delete an entry, it must be recreated as a new entry. You will be returned to the Address Book list.

In this lesson you learned how to make changes to existing address entries and how to delete address entries you no longer need. In the next lesson you will learn how to compose and send a fax message.

COMPOSING AND SENDING A FAX

In this lesson you will learn how to compose and send a fax message.

The ability to send and receive faxes directly through your computer or network with a fax modem is a powerful business tool. Think of a fax as a mail message which is sent over phone lines.

Faxes can be sent using several methods. For example, while in Exchange you can send a quick fax by creating a note on a cover page or you can attach existing files to a fax. You can fax directly from your application, attaching a cover page where desired. You can also send a fax from My Computer or the Windows Explorer. You'll learn how to send faxes using each of these methods in this lesson.

CREATING A FAX FROM THE EXCHANGE VIEWER

While in the Exchange Viewer, you can send a fax which includes a cover page and attached files. When the fax is sent, the recipient can edit the cover page and attached files if they received the fax through Windows 95 and Exchange.

STARTING THE FAX WIZARD

To send a fax from the Exchange Viewer, use these steps:

1. Choose Compose, New Fax. The Fax Wizard will start by displaying the Compose New Fax dialog box, as shown in Figure 14.1.

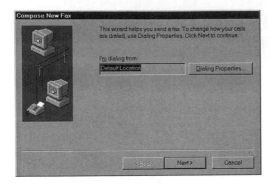

Figure 14.1   The Fax Wizard starts by allowing you to select an originating location.

2. If you are dialing from the location displayed, go to the next step. Otherwise, click the Dialing Properties button and select the correct location from the I am dialing from: drop-down list. See Figure 14.2.

If your dialing location is not displayed, you can add a new location also from the My Locations tab of the Dialing Properties dialog box. To add a new location, from the Dialing Properties dialog box, click New. Next, type a location name in the Create a new location named text box and click OK. The new location name will be added to the I am dialing from drop down list in the Dialing Properties dialog box. Refer to Figure 14.2 as you complete the new Dialing Properties location settings.

Complete each field to define the elements used when dialing from the new location. You'll need to enter your local area code and select a country code to identify how long distance calls should be placed. Then complete each remaining field which identify any special requirements for placing a call from your current location. For example, if you must dial 9 to access an outside line, whether calls must be placed using a calling card, the digits necessary to turn off call waiting, and whether your phone system uses tone or pulse dialing.

When your dialing location is correct, click OK.

Not using a portable computer?   The first time you use the Fax Wizard, or if you fax from a portable computer, an additional checkbox will appear toward the bottom of the Compose New Fax dialog box which suggests that you check the box if you are not using a portable computer and do not want to see the prompt again. If you are not using a portable computer, verify that the Dialing Properties for your location are correct, then click the checkbox I'm not using a portable computer so don't show this to me again. This will prevent the Location prompt from appearing each time you use the Fax Wizard.

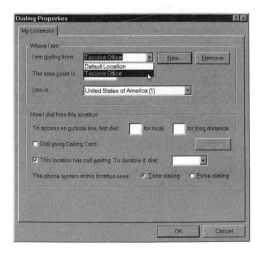

FIGURE 14.2   The Dialing Properties dialog box allows you to select, add, or remove dialing locations for faxes.

ADDRESSING THE FAX

Addressing the fax designates who the fax recipients are. You can type the recipient's name and fax numbers, or you can choose them from an address book.

Continue through the Fax Wizard prompt boxes using these steps:

1. Click the Next button to move to the Compose New Fax dialog box, displayed in Figure 14.3.

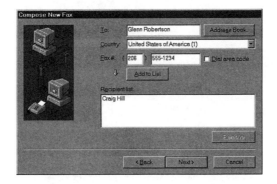

FIGURE 14.3 Address your fax from the Compose New Fax dialog box.

2. Click the Address Book button to choose names from your address book entries. Or, type the names and fax phone numbers for your fax recipients in the To text box. Click Add to List to add the name to the Recipient list.

3. If you type a name that is listed more than once in your address books, you will see the Check Names dialog box displayed in Figure 14.4. You can then either select a name from the list of displayed names in the Change to list, or create a new address entry by clicking Create a new address for... If several names are listed, the easiest method to verify the entry you want to use is to click the Properties button so that you can view the entry.

If you need to create a new address entry, click Create a new address for..., then click OK. Complete the new address entry using the same steps you used to create any other address entry. If you need to, review the steps in the section Adding New Fax Entries in Lesson 12. When your new entry is finished, click OK to continue with the Compose New Fax wizard.

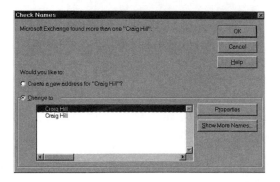

Figure 14.4   The Check Names dialog box appears if Exchange finds multiple addresses for your recipient.

Setting Cover Page Options

A cover page precedes the actual text of your fax message. It is usually used when you want to write a note to the recipient in addition to any other pages included with the fax. When the fax is sent, the cover page is sent first, then any attachments and fax text. Continue using the Fax Wizard, setting cover page options as follows:

1. When your recipient list is complete, click Next to move to the cover page prompt of the Fax Wizard, shown in Figure 14.5.

2. If you want to use a cover page for your fax, click the Yes, Send this one option button and select one from the displayed list. If you do not want to use a cover page, click No.

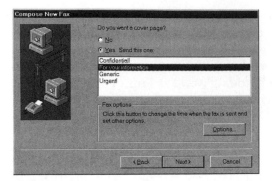

FIGURE 14.5 Select a cover page and set fax options from the Fax Wizard cover page prompt.

3. Options to send a fax at a designated time and security options, such as assigning *key encryption* or password-protected faxes, can also be chosen from the cover page prompt. If you want to delay the time your fax will be sent, or assign security options to the fax, choose the Options button, then complete the send and security options you need. When your options are complete, choose OK. You will be returned to the cover page prompt box.

4. Choose Next.

5. If you have chosen to include a cover page for your fax, you will see the dialog box shown in Figure 14.6. If you have not included a cover page, go to the next step. Type a subject line for your cover sheet, then click in the Note area and type any text you want to include on the cover page.

6. When complete, choose Next.

Key Encryption   An advanced level of fax security available only for editable faxes, key encryption scrambles the contents of a fax unless the recipient has a public *key* and knows your private key. Key encryption requires that Advanced Fax Security has been set up (through choosing Tools, Microsoft Fax Tools, Advanced Fax Security), and that public keys have been distributed to other Exchange users.

Keys are basically sets of passwords which are used to ensure that the recipient of a fax has the right to read or open a fax. Public keys are distributed among all fax recipients. Private keys are assigned to each individual and are not shared. When you send a key-encrypted fax, a combination of the recipient's public key and your private key are used to encrypt the fax message. Your private key assures the recipient that the fax could have only come from you. They then use their public key to unlock and read the fax.

FIGURE 14.6   A subject line and note will start on the cover page.

ATTACHING FILES TO YOUR FAX

Since you are creating your fax directly through Exchange, you will probably want to attach a file, or files, to the fax. If your recipient is not using Windows 95 Exchange also, the attached file will be *imaged* or *rendered* (converted into binary code) and sent as the fax.

 Imaging or Rendering Faxes which are generated from a computer and sent through a fax modem are typically imaged, or rendered. This means that a "picture" of the fax document is created in a proprietary graphic format which exactly duplicates the file's format. The imaged file is then sent as a fax.

To attach a file to your fax, continue with the Fax Wizard, following the next step:

1. To include a file with your fax, click the Add File button in the Fax Wizard dialog box (see Figure 14.7).

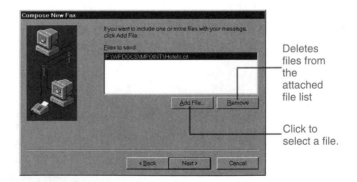

FIGURE 14.7 Attached files are listed in the Files to send text box.

2. Choose a file from the displayed file list, shown in Figure 14.8. You can move through your folders using the toolbar folder buttons. When you have chosen the file to

be included, choose Next. You will be returned to the Add
File prompt box.

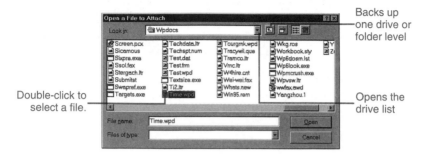

Double-click to
select a file.

Backs up
one drive or
folder level

Opens the
drive list

Figure 14.8   Select files from the Open a File to Attach dialog
box.

3. Repeat steps 1 and 2 for each file to be included with your
    fax. When all files have been selected, choose Next.

Sending the Fax

The last prompt through the Fax Wizard actually sends the fax
you just created to the fax modem. To complete the Fax Wizard
and send the fax: Click the Finish button. Fax Wizard will close
and the fax will be sent to your fax modem. If you have changed
the send time, the fax will be sent to your Outbox then submitted
to your fax modem at the correct time.

Sending a Fax Directly from an Application

Sending a fax directly from an application is efficient; however, it
probably isn't any faster. By faxing directly from an application,
however, the file you want to fax is already open. Therefore you
don't need to locate the file to be faxed as an attachment to a fax
message as you must do when you fax from within Exchange.

When Microsoft Fax Services is installed (follow the steps on the inside front cover to install if you've not done so), Exchange creates a printer driver named Microsoft Fax on FAX. This fax printer driver is added to your Printers list. When you print a file to the Microsoft Fax printer, the Fax Wizard starts, prompts you through the creation of a cover page and sends the fax.

For example, suppose you have created a spreadsheet in Excel and now want to fax it to another office for review. By printing the spreadsheet to the Microsoft Fax printer, the Fax Wizard begins, prompts you to add a cover page, then submits both the cover page and the spreadsheet to the fax modem.

While each application can differ slightly, the basic steps to send a fax from an application are similar:

1. From the application, select the Microsoft Fax printer. In a Windows 95 application, choose File, Print. Then select the Microsoft Fax on FAX from the Name drop-down list. (Your application might list the printer simply as Microsoft Fax.)

2. Complete any print parameters you need, such as a range of pages, then click OK. Fax Wizard will start.

3. You might need to select a dialing location. If so, select the location by clicking the Dialing Properties button, or click Next to accept the location displayed in the I'm dailing from text box. If you need to change the dialing location, review step 2 in the section titled "Starting the Fax Wizard" covered earlier in this lesson.

4. Complete the address information for the fax, then click Next.

5. Select a cover page, if desired, then click Next.

6. If you're including a cover page, type the subject text and any notes you want to include on the cover page. Then click Next to continue.

7. Choose Finish to send the fax.

SENDING A FAX FROM MY COMPUTER OR THE WINDOWS EXPLORER

To send a fax directly from My Computer or the Windows Explorer:

1. From a My Computer or Windows Explorer window, select the file to be faxed.

2. Right-click the mouse, then select Send To, Fax Recipient, as displayed in Figure 14.9. The Fax Wizard will start.

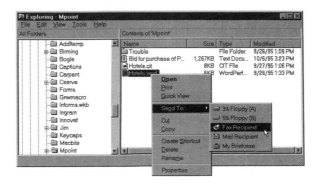

FIGURE 14.9   Faxes can be sent from a My Computer or Windows Explorer window.

3. Complete each prompt box for the Fax Wizard, choosing Next to step through each prompt in turn.

4. When all prompts are completed, choose Finish to send the selected files to the fax modem.

SENDING A FAX WITH THE START MENU OF WINDOWS 95

Yet one more method can be used to send a fax. Fax services are also available from the Windows 95 Start, Programs menu list. To start the Fax Wizard:

1. Choose Start from the Windows 95 taskbar.

2. Choose Programs, Accessories, Fax, Compose New Fax. The Fax Wizard will start.

3. Complete each prompt dialog box for the Fax Wizard, creating a cover page if desired, and attaching any necessary files.

In this lesson you learned how to compose and send a fax message. In the next lesson, you will learn how to receive, view, and print a fax message.

RECEIVING AND VIEWING A FAX IN EXCHANGE

15

In this lesson you will learn how to receive, view, and print a fax message.

Faxes you receive are listed in your Inbox. You can sometimes tell by looking at a received fax message whether the sender generated the fax from a dedicated fax machine, or whether the fax was created from a system equipped with a fax modem. If the fax was generated through a fax modem, the fax will appear in your Inbox as a message icon, with an attachment. If the fax was sent from a dedicated fax machine, it will appear in your Inbox as a fax machine icon (see Figure 15.1).

Fax generated from a fax modem

From	Subject	Received ▼	Size
72066,3035	Receipt of message	10/12/95 7:39 PM	1K
714 566 7705	Fax from 714 566 7705	10/12/95 3:01 PM	32K
Tech Data Corp	Fax from Tech Data Corp	10/12/95 10:31 AM	116K
John Chmela	VBDN October Meeting	10/10/95 4:40 AM	2K
206 473 7202	Fax from 206 473 7202	10/9/95 7:05 PM	388K
Bill Castle		10/6/95 2:28 PM	4K
Bill Castle	TRIPS.XLS	10/6/95 1:43 PM	77K
Bill Castle	Book1.xls	10/6/95 1:42 PM	16K
206 454 2045	Fax from 206 454 2045	10/6/95 10:18 AM	494K
Ed Mitchell	WURD PURFICT	10/5/95 5:49 PM	4K
Henry Simoen	Read: RE: More memory, please??	9/29/95 11:19 AM	2K

45 items

Fax generated through a dedicated fax machine

FIGURE 15.1 Received faxes appear in your Inbox list.

RECEIVING A FAX

Depending on the current answer options, typically chosen when Fax Services was installed, Fax Services will automatically answer

an incoming fax, prompt you to answer a call, or will not answer
a call. The default option for Exchange is to not answer fax calls.
See Lesson 17 to learn how to change the answering options.

MANUALLY ANSWERING AN INCOMING FAX CALL

When Fax Services is configured to manually answer incoming
fax calls, a dialog box will appear when an incoming call is de-
tected by your fax modem. You can choose to either answer the
fax call or to decline the call. You should be able to continue to
work while a fax is being received by your fax modem. If you are
using a slower system, however, you may experience some system
interruption while the fax modem is receiving the fax message.

Click the Yes button to instruct Fax Services to answer the call or
No to decline the call.

ANSWERING A FAX CALL WHEN FAX SERVICES IS CONFIGURED TO DON'T ANSWER

You can instruct Fax Services to answer a call even if it is configured not to. You may be able to hear the fax phone line ring
signalling that a fax is incoming. In that case, you can manually
instruct Fax Services to answer the fax call. This is especially useful if you want to answer a call using another computer system
which also has a fax modem and Fax Services.

For example, some small offices, like mine, have one computer
system which acts as a *fax server*. That system is configured to
answer all incoming fax calls. The received faxes are then routed
to each user's mailbox. Sometimes, however, the fax server system
is out of service—either it's not turned on or, for some reason,
doesn't answer the fax line when it is ringing. Since all of our user
systems have fax modems and Fax Services installed (to allow
faxes to be sent from any system), any one of us can manually
answer an incoming fax if the fax server misses the call for some
reason.

When Exchange is started with Fax Services installed, a fax icon appears in the Windows 95 taskbar as shown in Figure 15.2. To answer a call, click the fax icon in the taskbar and the Microsoft Fax Status dialog box appears. Click the Answer Now button.

Click here to manually answer an incoming fax.

FIGURE 15.2   The Microsoft Fax Status dialog box allows you to manually answer a fax call.

READING A FAX

Reading a fax is similar to reading any other message. Some faxes will appear as attachments to a message and must be opened as an attachment. Other faxes will open automatically when you choose the message. An opened fax is displayed using the Fax Viewer.

Faxes received from another Exchange user will appear as simple messages and can be edited, providing the other user has Exchange configured to send editable faxes. See Lesson 17 for more information about sending editable faxes.

OPENING A FAX

To open a fax, use these steps:

1. From the Inbox, select the fax message you want to open.

2. Double-click the message, or press Enter. If the message is an editable fax, the standard message window will open and you can read the fax just as you would any other message. More commonly, however, the Fax Viewer will open and display the fax message.

3. If the opened message contains an attachment, open the attachment by double-clicking the attachment icon.

MANIPULATING THE FAX TO MAKE IT EASIER TO READ ON-SCREEN

An opened fax can sometimes be difficult to read. When sent from a manual fax machine, fax pages can be fed into a manual fax machine in any order, sometimes even upside down. Therefore, the Fax Viewer has a specific toolbar and menu which contain functions used to manipulate the fax image. You can rotate a fax, invert the image, enlarge the display size by zooming the image in or out, and drag the fax image to a different location with the viewer. You can also print a fax, save it to a file, or even select and copy portions of a fax image for use in other applications. Thumbnails of a multiple page fax can also be displayed.

You can change the size of the fax image as it appears on-screen, using the zoom buttons. Use the buttons on the Fax Viewer toolbar to manipulate a fax.

VIEWING A DIFFERENT PAGE

If you have a long fax, you can quickly move to subsequent, or previous, pages of the fax by using the Next page/Previous page scroll bar buttons, or by selecting a displayed Thumbnail page. See Figure 15.3 to locate the Page and Thumbnail buttons.

To choose a page using thumbnails:

1. If not already displayed, turn on Thumbnail view by clicking the Thumbnail button from the Toolbar.

2. Click the Thumbnail image for the page you want to view on the left side of the screen. If you can't see the thumbnail of the page you want to view, use the scroll bars next to the thumbnails.

Click to view the previous page

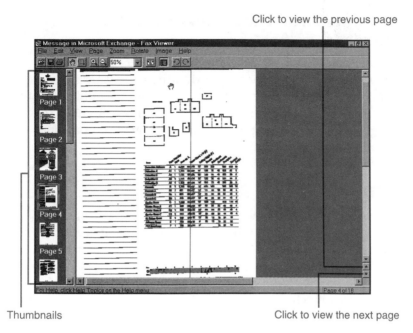

Thumbnails

Click to view the next page

FIGURE 15.3   Use buttons and thumbnails to quickly move from page to page.

MANIPULATING THE FAX IMAGE

Click the Rotate left or Rotate right toolbar buttons to rotate the fax image at 90-degree increments. Each time you click a rotate button, the image will pivot 90 degrees in the direction you have chosen. If you want to rotate the image 180 degrees, you can either click the Rotate left or Rotate right Toolbar buttons twice, or choose Rotate, Flip over.

To invert an image, so that it appears with black letters on a white background, or white letters on a black background, choose Image, Invert.

DRAGGING THE IMAGE WITHIN THE FAX VIEWER

The hand pointer is the default mouse pointer when the Fax Viewer is open. It is used to reposition the current fax image within the Fax Viewer. If the hand pointer is not visible, click the Drag toolbar button. Then drag the hand pointer to move the fax image. Release the hand pointer when the image is positioned on-screen where you want it.

PRINTING THE FAX

Printing a fax can be done from the Fax Viewer, or from the Inbox. Be aware, however, that if you have rotated or flipped the fax image while viewing it in the Fax Viewer, the printed copy of the fax will also be rotated or flipped. This might cause the fax to be printed sideways on a page, for example. To print a fax from the Fax Viewer, click the Print toolbar button. To print a fax from the Inbox, choose File, Print, or press Ctrl+B. Be sure to click the Print Attachments checkbox if your fax message contains an attachment.

In this lesson you learned how to receive, view, and print a fax message. In the next lesson you will learn how to work with the Fax Cover Page Editor, and how to create a fax cover page which includes graphics, text, and fax information fields.

CREATING A
CUSTOM FAX
COVER PAGE

*In this lesson you will learn how to
work with the Fax Cover Page Editor, and how to create a fax cover
page which includes graphics, text, and fax information fields.*

Microsoft's Fax Services installs with four pre-defined fax cover
pages. These cover pages, modifiable by you using the Fax Cover
Page Editor, can be sent as the first page of a fax transmission. The
pre-defined cover pages contain personal information (called fax
information fields) such as your name, company, address, phone
and fax numbers, along with the name of the person to whom
you are faxing, their fax number, and so on. You can use the Fax
Cover Page Editor to create your own cover page, or to edit an
existing cover page. Fax cover pages you define or edit can also
include these fields along with any other text or graphics you
want to add.

STARTING THE FAX COVER PAGE EDITOR

When Fax Services are installed, a shortcut to the Fax Cover Page
Editor is created in your Programs list. You can start the Fax Cover
Page Editor by using these steps:

1. Click Start from the Windows 95 taskbar.

2. Choose Programs.

3. Choose Accessories.

4. Choose Fax.

5. Choose Cover Page Editor.

UNDERSTANDING THE COVER PAGE EDITOR

The Fax Cover Page Editor contains buttons and menu selections similar to those used by most graphic or forms design products. As you can see in Figure 16.1, two toolbars are used to quickly access commands you will need when editing a cover page. Rest the mouse pointer on any of the buttons on either toolbar to view the ToolTip for the button. You'll find a complete list of all toolbar buttons on the inside back cover of this book. Review Figure 16.1 to locate the general button groups.

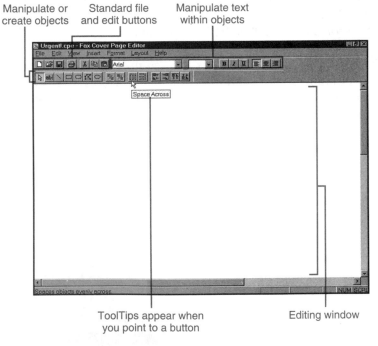

FIGURE 16.1 The buttons are grouped according to their functions.

THE PRE-DEFINED COVER PAGES

The four pre-defined cover pages are titled "Generic," "For your information," "Urgent," and "Confidential." You choose one of these four cover pages, or a custom page you've defined, whenever you use the Fax Wizard. Turn back to Lesson 14 if you need to review the steps used by the Fax Wizard.

 Custom Fax Cover Page   To create your own custom fax cover page, see the section titled "Creating a New Fax Cover Page" later in this lesson.

You can view and modify the appearance of any of the four pre-defined cover pages, or any cover pages you have defined, by opening their files. To do so from the Fax Cover Page Editor:

1. Choose File, Open, or click the Open button on the Toolbar. The Open dialog box will appear.

2. Select the fax cover page you want to open from the list of folders and files. Fax Cover Pages are saved with the extension .CPE and are usually in your Windows folder. You may need to change drives or folders to locate your cover pages. You may not be set up to see file extensions in Windows 95 unless you opted to see them. If you want to see file extensions, see your Windows documentation for instructions.

3. Click Open. The cover page you have selected will open in the Fax Cover Page Editor.

UNDERSTANDING THE FAX COVER PAGE ELEMENTS

Fax cover pages contain two element types: objects and text frames. An object is a graphic, drawing, or a fax information field. A text frame contains text that will appear every time you use the cover page. For example, the title phrase "Fax Cover Page" shown in Figure 16.2 is text within a text frame.

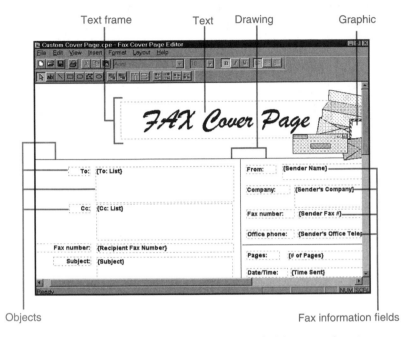

Figure 16.2   Cover pages are made up of objects and text frames.

The size of each element is defined by the dashed lines which surround the element. *Select* an element by pointing to an element and clicking. When selected, handles (small square boxes at the corners and centers of the element) appear which can be dragged to size the element (see Figure 16.3).

Select   Selecting an element chooses it so that it can be formatted, deleted, moved, sized or modified in some form. Deselect an object by clicking the mouse outside the element.

Sizing pointer   Handles

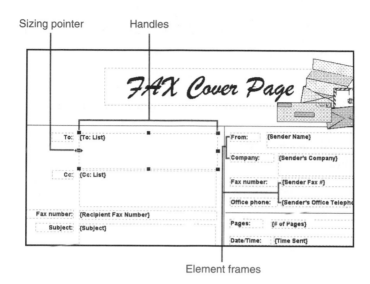

Element frames

FIGURE 16.3   A selected object has eight handles.

TIP   **Selecting Multiple Objects**   You can select several objects by clicking each object in turn while holding the Ctrl key. Alternately, drag the pointer around a group of objects. When you release the mouse button, each of the objects within the group will be selected.

You can also move the element to a new location by selecting it and dragging it to a new position. The pointer changes to a four-sided arrow when dragging. Release the mouse button when the element is correctly placed.

TIP   **Save**   Be sure to periodically save your cover page file while you are editing.

CREATING A NEW FAX COVER PAGE

If you are not completely happy with the pre-defined cover pages and editing them does not meet your needs, you can create your own fax cover page. You can use the following general steps in any order to create your new fax cover page. For information on each of the steps, see the subsequent sections.

1. If you have an existing fax cover page on-screen, first choose File, New.

2. Select a paper size for the page.

3. Create any objects or select them from existing files.

4. Add any text frames.

5. Add fax information fields.

6. Move and size any of the elements as necessary.

SETTING THE PAPER SIZE

Unless you specify otherwise, a new cover page is automatically created to the default paper definition for the Microsoft Fax printer (usually 8.5" by 11"). To select an alternate paper size for your cover sheet, use these steps:

1. Choose File, Page Setup.

2. Select the Microsoft Fax printer by clicking the Printer button, then selecting Microsoft Fax from the Printer pull-down list. Then click OK.

3. Select the paper size you want to use from the Size pull-down list, then click OK.

ADDING OBJECTS

Objects can be files which already exist, they can be new objects which you create, or they can be simple graphics created by using the drawing tool buttons. Creating a new object will open the object type's application within the Cover Page Editor. For example, if you want to create a WordPad object, WordPad will open within the Cover Page Editor. Then when the new object is complete, WordPad will close, leaving the new object in your cover page.

To create a new object, use these steps:

1. Choose Insert, Object.

2. Click Create New.

3. Select the object type you want to create from the Object Type list, then click OK. The Object Type list lists those objects for which you have applications on your own computer, or on your network if you are connected to a network. The application used to create the object will be opened within the Cover Page Editor.

4. Create your new object.

5. Close the application and add your object to your cover page by clicking outside the object.

You can also create new objects with the drawing tools. The drawing Toolbar can be used to draw lines, rectangles, rounded rectangles, polygons, and ellipses on your cover page. Each of these tools works similarly:

1. Click the tool button you want to use from the Toolbar.

2. Click and drag the mouse pointer to the shape you require.

3. Release the mouse button to stop. (You'll need to double-click the polygon tool when you're finished with it.) The object will appear in your cover page. You can size and move it as you need.

To add an existing object file to your cover page, use these steps:

1. Choose Insert, Object.

2. Click Create from File, then choose the file to be linked. (Click the Browse button to locate the file, if necessary.) Click OK when your choice is complete. The object will be added to the cover page.

ADDING TEXT FRAMES

Text frames contain text which is created using the text button on the cover page Toolbar. A *text frame* sets the space you want to use for the text on your cover page. You'll want to make your text frame large enough to contain all of your text. To create a text frame:

1. Click the Text button. The mouse pointer will change to crosshairs.

2. Click and drag the mouse pointer to the desired size for your text frame. Don't worry if you don't create a large enough text frame. You can easily resize it later by selecting the text frame and dragging one of the frame handles.

3. Type the text to be contained within the frame. Add any formatting you need by selecting the text and using the text Toolbar buttons.

4. Click outside the text frame when finished.

ADDING FAX INFORMATION FIELDS

Fax information fields are predefined by Fax Services. They are used to include identifying information for the sender and information about the recipient on the cover page. When the fields are added to a cover page and the cover page is selected when sending a fax, sender information comes from entries stored in the User tab in the Fax Setup dialog box. (See Lesson 17 for more about the User tab.) Recipient information comes from an address book entry. You can also include a fax information field which adds any message text you type when using the Fax Wizard to edit your cover page. At a minimum, you'll probably want to include the Sender Name, Sender Fax Number, and the Recipient Name information fields on your cover page.

Fax information fields are grouped by Recipient fields, Sender fields, and Message fields. To add a field, use these steps:

1. Choose Insert.

2. Choose between Recipient, Sender, or Message.

3. Choose the field you want to add. The field will be added to your cover page.

4. Position the field on your cover page by dragging it with the mouse.

5. Click outside the field to deselect it.

6. Repeat steps 1-5 for each field to be added.

ALIGNING AND POSITIONING OBJECTS ON THE PAGE

Positioning objects so that they all are evenly spaced or so that they line up neatly is also easy:

1. Select the objects to be aligned.

2. Click the spacing button, or alignment button you need (see Figure 16.4). The objects will adjust to the alignment or spacing option you have chosen.

Undo! If you don't like the changes you've made, you can easily undo them. Choose Edit, Undo, or press Ctrl+Z, to undo your last change. You can continue to undo your changes until the Undo choice is no longer available.

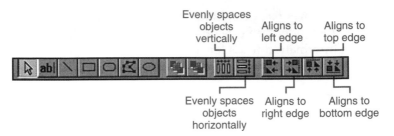

FIGURE 16.4   Alignment and spacing tools.

 TIP   **Stacking objects**   To have one object appear in front of or behind another object, use the Bring to Front or Send to Back tools.

In this lesson you learned how to work with the Fax Cover Page Editor, and how to create a fax cover page which includes graphics, text, and fax information fields. In the next lesson you will learn how to set options for answering and delivering fax messages. You will also learn how to change the mailbox to which faxes are delivered and other user information for cover pages.

CHANGING FAX OPTIONS

In this lesson you will learn how to set options for answering and delivering fax messages. You will also learn how to change the mailbox to which faxes are delivered and other user information for cover pages.

Many fax options are set when Exchange Fax Services is installed. As you work with Fax Services you may need to modify some of those settings. The fax options allow you to modify settings such as:

- Whether an incoming call is automatically answered by Fax Services.

- Whether you want to include a cover page with sent faxes by default and, if so, which one.

- What action Fax Services should take if a busy signal occurs when attempting to send a fax.

- What return fax number should be included on a cover page.

- Which modem should be used when sending or receiving a fax.

All Fax Service options are set or modified through the Microsoft Fax Properties dialog box. There are two routes available from the Exchange Viewer to access this dialog box.

- Choose Tools, Microsoft Fax Tools, Options.

- Choose Tools, Options. Then select Microsoft Fax from the list of installed services and click on the Properties button.

The Microsoft Fax Properties dialog box will appear as displayed in Figure 17.1.

FIGURE 17.1   The Microsoft Fax Properties dialog box allows you to change Fax Service options.

To move from one tab to another, simply click on the tab at the top of the Microsoft Fax Properties dialog box. When you have completed your default setting changes in the tabs, click OK to return to the Exchange Viewer. If you've made changes to your fax modem settings, you'll be notified that the changes you've made will not take effect until you restart Exchange. If you receive this message, be sure to close Exchange, then start it again. The rest of this lesson will show you how to change the settings.

USING THE MESSAGE TAB

The Message Tab is open or on top when you access the Microsoft Fax Properties dialog box. This tab is used to set options for fax messages you send. You can tell Fax Services to send faxes at a given time, select a default cover page or create a new one, and choose the default message format. The Message Tab also determines whether you will be able to edit the subject line of faxes which you receive. This is especially useful when forwarding a fax.

SETTING THE TIME TO SEND A FAX

Faxes are usually sent immediately after Fax Wizard finishes. You can choose to send your faxes at a particular time, or when discount rates apply. To change the time when faxes are sent, from the Message Tab click the Time to Send option button you want to use. To specify when discount rates apply:

1. From the Message Tab, click the Set button.

2. Set the time range used for discount calling rates.

3. Click OK to return to the Message Tab.

SELECTING COVER PAGE CHOICES

The Default cover page section of the Message Tab is used to tell Fax Wizard whether you want to use a cover page by default, and if so, which cover page. You can also start the Fax Cover Page Editor from this section, creating a new cover page or editing an existing one.

You can use these choices for fax cover pages:

Send cover page   Check this box, then select a cover page from the list which follows.

New   Click the New button to create a new fax cover page. The Fax Cover Page Editor will open, allowing you to create and save a new cover page. Review Lesson 16 for help in creating fax cover pages.

Open   Select a fax cover page from the list, then click the Open button. The fax cover page you selected will open in the Fax Cover Page Editor so that you can make any changes you need. Review Lesson 16 for help in editing fax cover pages.

Browse   Click the Browse button if you want to look for a cover page which is not listed in the cover page list box. You will be taken to the Browse Cover Page dialog box which, similar to most Windows 95 file and folder displays, allows you to look through various folders and drives. When you find the fax cover page to be added to the list, click the Open button. You will be returned to the Message tab of the Microsoft Fax Properties dialog box and the selected fax cover page will appear in the list box.

SETTING MESSAGE FORMAT OPTIONS

Message format options determine whether the recipient of your fax message can edit your fax message. Even if you choose to allow editing, the recipient will only be able to do so if they also use Microsoft Fax services. If they do not use Microsoft Fax, your message will be received by them as a *bitmap image*.

Bitmap image   Bitmap images are graphics which are created using columns and rows of dots. They are often somewhat ragged, or jagged, in appearance. Bitmaps are also sometimes referred to as *raster* graphics. Most bitmap images can be edited using some type of paint software, such as Microsoft Paint. When you edit a bitmap image, you add to or remove dots from the image. The bitmap image created by Microsoft Fax is proprietary and cannot be edited by other graphic software.

Three choices are available for setting message format:

Editable, if possible is the installed default setting for Microsoft Fax. This choice creates a fax which is editable by those users who receive a fax and also use Microsoft Fax services. If the users do not use Microsoft Fax services, the fax will be a bitmap image.

Choose **Editable only** if you know that the persons to whom you are sending your faxes will receive the fax using Microsoft Fax services. If you choose this option and the fax recipient does not have Microsoft Fax, the fax will not be readable by the recipient.

Sending faxes in **Not editable** format forces all faxes to be sent as bitmap images. While all recipients can read a bitmap fax, those recipients who use Microsoft Fax services will not be able to edit the fax.

Click the message format options you want your messages to use. You can also select a new default paper size to be used for your fax messages (the default is Letter size, 8 1/2 × 11 inches) by clicking the Paper button and selecting a size.

USING THE DIALING TAB

The Dialing Tab sets the options used by Fax Services when dialing the recipient's fax number. For example, if Fax Services encounters a busy signal, it will automatically redial 5 times (the default is 3 times), pausing 2 minutes between tries. To change the retry options, click in each retry box, typing the number of retries and the time between the retries you want to use.

You can also add dialing settings such as whether to dial using a calling card by clicking the Dialing Properties button and completing its associated dialog box. You'll want to be sure and set the dialing properties Fax Services that you most regularly use to send faxes from your computer. If you're setting up Exchange on a portable computer that often dials from different locations, you'll want to also create a profile for each location from which you send faxes. You'll learn more about creating profiles and customizing Fax Services in Lessons 21 and 22.

SETTING LONG DISTANCE PREFIXES

The Toll Prefixes button is used to select those prefixes (the first three digits of your telephone number) which are toll calls. This is useful if your area code contains several prefixes, some of which are long distance and others which are local calls. Refer to your telephone directory for a section which lists local and toll call prefixes. To set the toll prefixes for Fax Services:

1. From the Dialing Tab, click the Toll Prefixes button. You will see the dialog box shown in Figure 17.2.

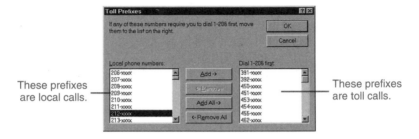

These prefixes are local calls.   These prefixes are toll calls.

FIGURE 17.2   Toll Prefixes are used to determine local and long distance calls.

2. From the Local phone numbers column, double-click on each prefix which is a toll call from your location. It will be added to the toll prefix column. If you double-click a number from the toll prefix column, it will be returned to the local prefix column.

3. When all prefixes have been chosen, click OK to return to the Dialing Tab, then click OK again to return to Exchange Viewer.

USING THE MODEM TAB

The Modem Tab sets options for automatic answering of incoming fax calls, and how Fax Services should handle outgoing calls. You can also choose an alternate fax modem, if you have more than one installed, and whether to share your fax modem with other users on your network.

SELECTING A FAX MODEM

A fax modem must first be installed in Windows 95 before it can be selected. Modems are installed through the Windows Control Panel, Modem utility. After modems are installed, they will be listed in the Modem Tab. To choose the modem you want Fax Services to use, select the modem in the Available fax modems list, then click the Set as Active Fax Modem button.

SETTING ANSWER OPTIONS

Fax Services does not automatically answer fax calls by default. You can change the answer options so that calls are answered on a designated ring, or so that the manual answer dialog box appears whenever the fax line rings. Fax Services can also be instructed not to answer any fax calls. To change the answer options for Fax Services, use these steps:

1. Click the Properties button from the Modem Tab. The Fax Modem Properties dialog box will appear.

2. Click the answer option you want to use in the Answer mode section. If you want Fax Services to automatically answer a call, open the Answer after rings drop-down list and select the number of rings which must occur before the call is answered.

3. If you want to change the speaker volume sound when Fax Services answers or sends a fax, drag the volume slide left or right. If you drag the slide to Off, no sound will be heard; the closer the slide appears to Loud, the greater the volume will be when a fax is sent or answered.

4. The default settings used in the Call preferences area are usually okay for most fax modems. Typically you'll want to always instruct your fax modem to wait for a dial tone before attempting to dial a fax, and you'll want the fax modem to hang up and wait if a busy tone is encountered when a fax number has been dialed. You can click the checkboxes next to each choice to check or uncheck the preferences for dialing.

5. Type the number of seconds you want Fax Services to wait for an answer when a fax number has been dialed in the After dialing, wait ... seconds for answer box. Be sure that your setting is large enough to allow for an answer by the receiving fax machine or fax modem. For example, if you often send faxes to a fax machine that is slow to answer, you should set the number of seconds to at least 60, or possibly 75 seconds.

Make any other changes desired, then click OK. You will be returned to the Fax Properties dialog box.

SETTING USER INFORMATION WITH THE USER TAB

Information in the User Tab is used by the Fax Wizard when completing a fax cover page, if the fax cover page contains the associated fax information fields (see Lesson 16). If your fax modem is shared, be sure to name the mailbox to which faxes should be delivered when received. To make changes to the user information:

1. Click the User Tab from the Microsoft Fax Properties dialog box. The User Tab will open.

2. Complete each text box, as indicated by the prompt text. You'll need to first click in the text box, then type the information. A brief explanation of each text box is listed immediately after this step. When you are finished, click OK to return to the Exchange Viewer.

Your full name Type your full name, or the name you want to include on a fax cover page in this text box.

Country If placed on a fax cover sheet, this field tells other users the country code they must use if they want to send you a fax from another country.

Fax number Your fax number, including the area code, can appear on a fax cover sheet.

Mailbox   The mailbox you type here will tell Fax Services where to deliver faxes which are addressed to you. If you did not install Fax Services yourself, you should contact your system administrator to learn the name of your mailbox.

Company, Address, Title, Department, Office Location and telephone numbers   The information you type in these fields can all appear on a fax cover sheet.

In this lesson, you learned how to set options for answering and delivering fax messages. You also learned how to change the mailbox to which faxes are delivered and user information for cover pages. In the next lesson, you will learn how to use Exchange without being logged on to your network, how to create mail for a remote session, how to pick up and send messages using remote mail, and how to schedule remote sessions.

18

USING REMOTE MAIL AND DIAL-UP NETWORKING

In this lesson you will learn how to use Exchange without being logged on to your network, how to create mail for a remote session, how to pick up and send messages using Remote Mail, and how to schedule remote sessions.

Dial-Up Networking is used by Windows 95 whenever you want your system to connect to another system using a modem and phone line. For example, you can use Dial-Up Networking to check your mail when you are on the road with a portable computer. You'll configure your portable computer to dial-up your office computer and transfer any messages you may have received, or those you may have created. Dial-Up Networking is also used by The Microsoft Network to define its connection information. You might also use Dial-Up Networking to define a connection to the Internet.

Windows 95 refers to a Dial-Up Networking Exchange session as Remote Mail. Dial-Up Networking must be installed on both your office system and your *remote* or *portable* system. Refer to Appendix A for instructions on installing Dial-Up Networking.

USING EXCHANGE OFFLINE

When you use your computer at work, Exchange automatically senses that you are logged on to your network and delivers messages based on your delivery schedule (usually every 10 minutes). When you use your portable computer away from the office, however, you are not usually connected to your network until you use your modem to dial into your system at work. This is referred to as working *offline*.

Working offline is exactly like working when connected to another system with the exception that you cannot transfer mail, or access files on the other system until you are online.

By default Exchange automatically detects whether you are connected to your LAN (Local Area Network) each time you start Exchange. If your network cannot be found, you are prompted to connect to your network using Remote services, or to work offline, as displayed in Figure 18.1.

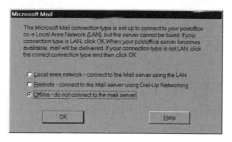

FIGURE 18.1   You are prompted to work Offline or via Remote if your LAN is not available.

If your portable computer will usually be used offline, you can configure Exchange so that it does not look for the network each time you open the Exchange Viewer. Use these steps:

1. From the Exchange Viewer, choose Tools, Services.

2. Select Microsoft Mail, then click Properties. The Microsoft Mail properties dialog box will appear as shown in Figure 18.2. The Connection tab is usually on top when the Microsoft Mail properties dialog box opens. If it is not on top, click the Connection tab.

3. Click the Offline option button to change your default Exchange startup option. Note that you can also change your default setting by clicking the Remote using a modem and Dial-Up Networking option button. If you

choose to do so, however, a dial-up connection will be attempted by Exchange each time it is started. This can be disruptive if you are not ready to connect, such as if you only wanted to review messages you previously received.

4. Click OK and OK again to return to the Exchange Viewer.

Select your
default
Exchange
startup
connection
here.

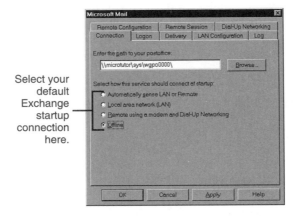

FIGURE 18.2   The Microsoft Mail properties dialog box allows you to choose default Mail settings.

CREATING AND READING MESSAGES OFFLINE

The steps used to create or read a message offline are the same steps you use when you are connected to your Mail postoffice. Messages you received during a Remote Mail session will appear in your Inbox. You can open the message by double-clicking on the message header in the Inbox.

Any messages you compose and send while offline remain in your Outbox until you connect to your network. When you use Remote Mail, the messages are sent to your Mail postoffice for delivery.

To create a message while you are offline:

1. From the Exchange Viewer, choose Tools, Compose New
   Message, press Ctrl+N, or click the New Message toolbar
   button.

2. Address, compose, and send your message using the same
   steps you learned in Lesson 5. The message will be sent to
   your Outbox.

Using Remote Mail to Transfer Mail

If you usually work offline, you will need to manually instruct
Exchange to dial-up your postoffice to send or receive mail. You
can transfer mail using either the Remote Mail command or by
choosing Deliver Now. Both are started from the Tools menu.

Transferring Mail Using Remote Mail

Transferring mail sends mail to and picks up mail from another
system while connected using Remote Mail. Your portable system,
in this case, is the *remote* system. The system to which you connect, usually the one at work, is called the *host* system.

Transferring mail is most effectively handled by using message, or
Mail, headers. Message or Mail headers are the same in Remote
Mail as they are when working with Exchange online. The header
displays identifying information for a message, such as the message subject, the date and time the message was received, who the
message was from, and so on. You can learn more about headers
by reviewing Lessons 3 and 22.

To transfer mail between the remote system and the host system,
use the following steps:

1. From the Exchange Viewer, choose Tools, Remote Mail.
   The Remote Mail-Microsoft Mail dialog box shown in
   Figure 18.3 will appear.

Delete this message.

Retrieve this message.

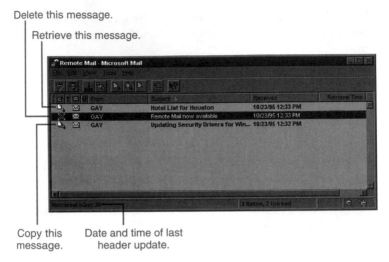

Copy this   Date and time of last
message.   header update.

Figure 18.3 The Remote Mail dialog box is used to mark messages and connect to your Postoffice.

2. If you have previously downloaded message headers, you can mark those messages you want to retrieve. First, click the message you want to mark, then click the Retrieve or Mark to retrieve a copy toolbar button.

3. When you are ready to transfer messages, click the Connect Toolbar button, or choose Tools, Connect and Transfer Mail. You can alternatively choose Tools, Connect and Update Headers.

4. Exchange will ask you to verify which connection you want to use to dial up your Mail server. If the appropriate connection is not displayed, select the correct one from the connection drop-down list. Then click OK.

5. Remote Mail will then connect to your network. If your postoffice resides on a secured network system such as Windows NT or Novell Netware, you will be prompted to type your network login name and your password.

When complete, click OK. You will see a prompt that tells you that you have connected to your computer and all mail will be transferred. When transfer is complete, Remote Mail will disconnect and you will be returned to the Exchange Viewer.

TRANSFERRING MAIL USING DELIVER NOW

An alternate method of transferring mail is through the Deliver Now choice under the Tools menu. As in delivering mail when working on your system at work, Deliver Now forces mail to be delivered from the Mail postoffice to each individual mailbox. When you are working offline, however, Deliver Now must perform a Dial-Up Networking/Remote Mail connection before the mail can be delivered. When you use Deliver Now, therefore, Remote Mail will dial-up your selected Dial-Up Networking connection, then transfer mail.

Deliver Now does not allow you to selectively mark any previously received mail headers for retrieval. It does, however, provide you with a list of choices for mail delivery. To use Deliver Now, follow these steps:

1. From the Exchange Viewer, choose Tools, Deliver Now Using, then select Microsoft Mail. Mail will display the Connect to Server dialog box shown in Figure 18.4.

2. Verify the connection to be used for Dial-Up Networking, or, if necessary, choose an alternate connection from the drop-down list box.

3. Click those activities you want Mail to perform while connected, such as sending or receiving mail. Be sure to click the Disconnect checkbox so that you do not remain online when the mail transfer is complete.

4. Click OK to begin the connection. If necessary, Mail will ask you to type your network logon and password, then (if instructed to do so in the Connect to Server dialog box) it will check for any new messages and will transfer messages from your Outbox to the Mail server. When transfer is complete, Mail will disconnect.

Choose an alternate connection definition here.

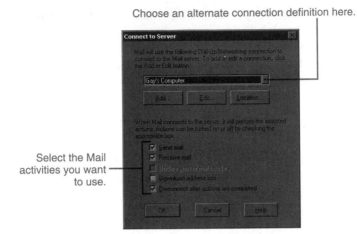

Select the Mail
activities you want
to use.

FIGURE 18.4   Deliver Now allows you to select Mail options from the Connect to Server dialog box.

SETTING MAIL TO AUTOMATICALLY CONNECT REMOTE MAIL

You can also configure Remote Mail to automatically connect to your Mail server at specific times to transfer mail. You can use one of the following routes to add a scheduled session:

1. From the Exchange Viewer, choose Tools, Microsoft Mail Tools.

2. Now choose Schedule Remote Mail Delivery. The Remote Scheduled Sessions dialog box will appear.

3. Click the Add button to add a new scheduled session. The Add Scheduled Session dialog box will appear.

Alternatively, you can use these steps:

1. From the Exchange Viewer choose Tools, Services.

2. Select Microsoft Mail, then click Properties.

3. Click the Remote Session Tab, then click the Schedule

Mail Delivery button. You will see the Remote Scheduled Session dialog box.

4. Choose Add to create a session schedule. The Add Scheduled Session dialog box will appear.

Now, complete the Add Scheduled Session dialog box using these steps:

1. Select the connection, time increment, and time of day to be used for Remote Mail.

2. Click OK to return to the Remote Scheduled Session dialog box. Your newly scheduled session will be listed.

3. Click OK, then OK again to return to the Exchange Viewer.

In this lesson you learned how to to use Exchange without being logged onto a network, how to create mail for a remote session, how to pick up and send messages using remote mail, and how to schedule remote sessions. In the next lesson you will learn how to send and receive e-mail from The Microsoft Network, how to locate addresses for other members, and how to add member addresses to your Personal Address Book.

USING THE MICROSOFT NETWORK FOR E-MAIL

In this lesson you will learn how to send and receive e-mail from The Microsoft Network, how to locate addresses of other members, and how to add member addresses to your Personal Address Book.

You can use The Microsoft Network (MSN) to transfer e-mail messages. Messages you receive from MSN will appear in your Exchange Inbox and can be read, replied to, and forwarded the same as any other message. Similarly, messages you compose and send will be listed in your Sent Items folder. You can also add MSN member addresses to your Personal Address Book.

What is MSN? MSN is an online service that comes with Windows 95. Through MSN you are able to perform typical online tasks. In addition, you can use MSN as a means of accessing the Internet and its e-mail and newsgroups. One of the best features of MSN is that, as a member, you will automatically receive e-mail notification of any updates or enhancements for Windows 95.

COMPOSING A MESSAGE FOR A MEMBER OF THE MICROSOFT NETWORK

You can compose a message to an MSN member either online or offline. You will need to know that member's ID so that you can properly address your message.

If you know the MSN member's ID, it is easiest to create a message for an MSN member while you are not signed on. You can then compose the message using the usual steps you have learned about in Exchange. As with any other message, if you attempt to send a message to a user whose address does not exist in an Address Book, you'll be prompted to create an address entry. You'll learn how to add an MSN member's ID to your address book later in this lesson. Review the steps in Lesson 5 if you need help sending messages.

COMPOSING AND DELIVERING A MESSAGE WHILE SIGNED ON WITH MSN

You can also compose a message while you are signed on with MSN. Use these steps:

1. Right-click the connection indicator on the Windows 95 Taskbar, then select Send Mail. The New Message dialog box will appear.

2. Compose your message, then click the Send toolbar button.

3. Choose Tools, Deliver Now Using.

4. Select Microsoft Network. The message will be delivered while you are signed on. At the same time, any messages to you will be delivered to your Inbox.

LOCATING AN MSN MEMBER ID AND ADDING IT TO YOUR PERSONAL ADDRESS BOOK

The address portion of your message must contain an MSN member ID. What if you don't know a member's ID? You can quickly locate a member ID and place it in your Personal Address Book, using these steps:

1. From the Exchange Viewer, choose Tools, Address Book.

2. Select Microsoft Network from the Show Names from the drop-down list.

3. Type the first few letters of the member name in the Type Name or Select from List: box. If you are offline, the Sign In dialog box for MSN will appear.

4. Verify or type your member ID and password, then click the Connect button. Your computer will dial MSN and you will see the address list starting with the letters you typed for the member to whom you want to send a message.

5. Click the address you want to use for your message, then click the Add to Personal Address Book toolbar button. See Figure 19.1.

Multiple Names Select several names to be added to your Personal Address Book by pressing Ctrl while you click on each name entry.

Click to add to your
Personal Address Book.

Click to select from
address book lists.

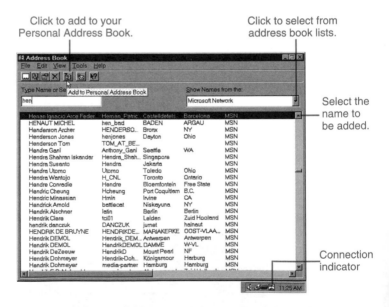

FIGURE 19.1 The Microsoft Network Address Book lists all members.

6. If you have finished with MSN, sign out of MSN by double-clicking the connection indicator in the Taskbar, then click the Yes button.

DELIVERING AND RECEIVING MSN MESSAGES

Transferring mail using MSN is quick and easy. You can send or receive mail while signed on to MSN, or you can sign-on, transfer mail, then immediately sign off.

To transfer mail while already signed on to MSN, use these steps:

1. Return to the MSN Central window by right-clicking the connection indicator and selecting MSN Central. See Figure 19.2 to view MSN Central.

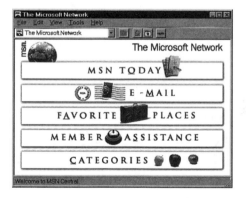

FIGURE 19.2   MSN Central is used to access all areas of MSN.

2. Click E-mail. The Exchange Viewer will open.

3. From the Exchange Viewer, choose Tools, Deliver Now Using.

4. Select The Microsoft Network.

To deliver mail while not signed on to MSN, use these steps:

1. From the Exchange Viewer, choose Tools, Deliver Now Using, The Microsoft Network. The MSN sign-in window will appear.

2. Verify that your member ID and password are correct, then click the Connect button. MSN will connect and your messages will be delivered. Messages to you will be received and listed in your Inbox.

3. If you are still online after message transfer is complete, right-click the connection indicator, then choose Sign Out. MSN will disconnect and you will be returned to the Exchange Viewer.

SCHEDULING EXCHANGE TO AUTOMATICALLY TRANSFER MSN MESSAGES

If you regularly use Exchange for e-mail messages to and from MSN, it can be especially useful to schedule an automatic dial-up session for mail transfer. Scheduled connections can occur every day at specific time increments, daily at a specific time, or just once on a date and time you define.

The easiest method to schedule an automatic mail transfer for MSN uses these steps:

1. From the Exchange Viewer, choose Microsoft Mail Tools. Then select Schedule Remote Mail Delivery. The Remote Scheduled Sessions dialog box will appear.

2. Click the Add button to open the Add Scheduled Session dialog box.

3. Select The Microsoft Network from the Use drop-down list.

4. Select the increment type you want to use from the When drop-down list. Choose one of the following:

   Every Every allows you to schedule a mail transfer at a time interval every day, such as every 6 hours, 30 minutes.

Weekly   Weekly displays a checkbox list of each day of the week, Sunday through Saturday, along with a time the mail transfer should start on the days you selected. Check those days you want mail transfer to occur. Then enter or select the time the mail transfer should start.

Once   Use once if you want to schedule a specific mail transfer time which will occur only one time. This is useful, for example, if you are going on vacation and want your mail to be transferred only once while you are away. You will need to supply both a date and time for the mail transfer to occur.

5. When your schedule is complete, click OK to return to the Remote Scheduled Sessions dialog box. Then click OK and OK again to return to the Exchange Viewer.

In this lesson you learned how to send and receive e-mail from The Microsoft Network, how to locate and use addresses for other members. In the next lesson you will learn how to add CompuServe as a Mail service in Exchange and how to send and receive mail from the Internet and CompuServe.

ADDING ONLINE SERVICES TO YOUR EXCHANGE PROFILE

In this lesson you will learn how to add CompuServe as a Mail service in Exchange. You will also learn how to send and receive mail from the Internet and CompuServe.

As you learned in the previous lessons, Microsoft Mail, Microsoft Fax and The Microsoft Network (MSN) are information services which are typically included when Exchange is installed. You can additionally add CompuServe and Internet as mail delivery services providing you have purchased the CD-ROM version of Windows 95, and Windows Plus! Exchange can communicate with other mail delivery systems as long as they are *MAPI* compliant. This means that the mail delivery system must follow the specifications used by the Messaging Application Programming Interface. As of the writing of this book, neither America OnLine nor Prodigy was MAPI compliant.

USING COMPUSERVE WITH EXCHANGE

CompuServe is only one of the more popular online services. If you have a CompuServe account, Exchange can access your account and transfer mail. Before you can use CompuServe in Exchange, it must be added as a mail delivery service.

ADDING COMPUSERVE TO EXCHANGE AS A MAIL SERVICE

The CompuServe messaging application for Exchange is included on the Windows 95 CD-ROM. Before you add CompuServe Mail to Exchange, you must know...

- Where on your system your existing CompuServe access software resides

- Your CompuServe telephone access number

- The name used for your CompuServe account

- Your CompuServe user ID

- Your CompuServe password

If you are already using WinCim or CompuServe Navigator, you can look in one of its Session Setting menus to locate your access number, account name and user ID. When you have gathered all the necessary information, use these steps to add CompuServe Mail to Exchange:

1. Close Exchange if it is open, then open the Windows Control Panel by clicking the Start button, then Settings, and then Control Panel.

2. Double-click the Mail and Fax icon. The MS Exchange Settings Properties dialog box will appear, similar to Figure 20.1.

3. Click Add, then click Have Disk.

4. Insert the Windows 95 Install CD in your CD-ROM drive, then click Browse.

5. Select your CD-ROM drive designation from the list, then select Drivers, Other, Exchange, Compusrv. Then click OK. The directory location will appear in the Install Other Information Service dialog box, similar to Figure 20.2.

6. Click OK. The CompuServe Mail files will be copied to your system. When complete, you will be asked if you want to add CompuServe Mail to your default profile.

FIGURE 20.1   The MS Exchange Settings Properties dialog box displays installed information services.

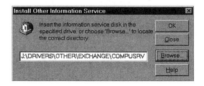

FIGURE 20.2   The Exchange CompuServe Mail service is located at \DRIVERS\OTHER\EXCHANGE\COMPUSRV on the Windows 95 CD-ROM.

7. Click Yes. The Inbox Setup Wizard will then start, asking you the current path to your existing CompuServe software.

8. Click Browse to select the correct drive and directory. If you are not using CompuServe software, select the drive and directory you want to use for possible CompuServe scripts or address books. When you have selected the drive and directory, click OK to write the location to the Inbox Setup Wizard.

9. Click Next to continue. The Inbox Setup Wizard will then prompt you for your Name, User ID, Password and access phone number.

10. Complete each field, then click Next.

11. Now check those CompuServe Mail options you want to use. (Uncheck those options you do not want.) You can choose from creating an activity log, deleting from CompuServe any messages retrieved by Exchange, or whether to accept any postage-due mail. When you are satisfied with your options, click Next.

12. The Inbox Setup Wizard now asks whether you want to include the Inbox in your Windows 95 Startup group. (This prompt box appears even if Exchange already starts automatically when Windows 95 starts.) If you want to add the Inbox to the Startup group, click the option to do so. Note that if it already exists in the Startup group, it will be added a second time!

13. You will be returned to the Add Service to Profile dialog box.

14. Since you earlier told the Inbox Setup Wizard that you wanted to add CompuServe Mail to your default profile, click Cancel to return to the MS Exchange Settings Properties box. Then click OK to return to the Control Panel. CompuServe will appear in your default profile when you next start Exchange.

CREATING AND TRANSFERRING MAIL USING COMPUSERVE MAIL

After installing CompuServe, you can compose and send messages to other CompuServe members after creating an entry in your address book. You'll then use that entry as the message address. To create an address book entry for a CompuServe member, use these steps:

1. From the Exchange Viewer, click the Address Book Toolbar button. The Address Book will open.

2. Click the New Entry button on the Toolbar.

3. Select CompuServe from the Entry type list, then click OK. Note that you can also use CompuServe as a gateway, or route, to many other online services such as SprintMail, MCI Mail or cc:Mail. You can select any of the other services listed, creating an address entry which will be used to send a message to another service using CompuServe as the delivery agent.

4. Type the name of the user in the Display Name box. The entry you type here will be the name which will appear in your address book list.

5. Type the CompuServe member ID in the E-Mail address box. CompuServe addresses usually appear as a series of 5-6 digits, a comma, then 3-4 additional digits: 101000,1234.

6. Type any comments you want to store with the entry, then click OK to return to the Address Book. If you are through with the Address Book, close it by clicking the Windows 95 close button.

To transfer mail to and from a CompuServe member, first compose and send the message as you normally would. Be sure to use the CompuServe address for the addressee. When the message is sent it will, as usual, remain in your Outbox until delivered. Now deliver the message by choosing Tools, Deliver Now Using, CompuServe Mail from the Exchange Viewer. Any messages you have composed will be delivered to CompuServe and any messages waiting for you will be delivered to your Inbox.

Only receiving some messages? Exchange only transfers mail to and from the Mail area of CompuServe, not any of CompuServe's individual forums where you might also receive or create messages. To receive messages from these areas you will still need to use one of CompuServe's other interfaces such as WinCIM®.

SENDING AND RECEIVING INTERNET MAIL

Internet messages can be transferred using either CompuServe or The MicroSoft Network. By using an Internet address in your message, MSN or CompuServe will deliver mail to an Internet address. Similarly, other users can use the Internet to send messages to you. Your own MSN Internet address is written as your MSN member ID@MSN.COM. For example, JohnS@MSN.COM. Your CompuServe Internet address is written as your CompuServe member ID@Compuserve.COM. For example, 123456.1234@ Compuserve.COM.

When you send an Internet message to another user, you'll need to know their exact Internet address. Then preface the address with INTERNET. For example, an Internet message might use the address INTERNET:JamesM@SRG.COM or INTERNET: SarahHM@ABC.COM.

To send an Internet message using either CompuServe or MSN, therefore, first create an address book entry which includes the word INTERNET: at the beginning of the e-mail address. (Be sure to include the colon (:) at the end of the word INTERNET, and note that there are no spaces within the address.) Then compose and send the message. The message will reside in your Outbox until you deliver the message using Deliver Now in the Tools menu.

ADDING AN INTERNET MAIL SERVICE

Internet Mail can be set up as an independent mail service. If you only want to send and receive Internet mail messages using Exchange and you are also using CompuServe or MSN, you do not need to install and use Internet Mail. Refer to the previous section titled "Sending and Receiving Internet Mail."

Internet Mail is used when you have an *Internet Server*. An Internet Server is used to connect a company's network server directly to the Internet, thus providing a direct method of routing mail without using an online service such as MSN, CompuServe or AOL. To use Internet Mail through Windows 95 Exchange, you must purchase and install Internet Services through Microsoft Plus!, a separate software package. Once you have installed and configured Internet Services, you can set up Internet Mail as an independent mail service on Exchange.

Even if you do not use the Internet Mail function of Plus!, you might wish to install its Internet Jumpstart kit so that you can use other Internet services such as the ability to dial up MSN's Internet service, browse Internet newsgroups or search for information.

Installing Internet Mail is a complex task, well beyond the scope of this book. One reference for installing Internet Mail is the *Special Edition Using Windows 95* also by Que. Once installed and properly configured, Internet Mail can automatically transfer messages throughout the day on a regular schedule. In general, you will need to do the following to install Internet Mail:

1. Install the Microsoft Plus! Internet Jumpstart Kit. The Internet Setup Wizard will prompt you through several basic settings used to start Internet services from your Windows 95 installation.

2. Install Dial-Up Networking on your system.

3. Bind and configure the Windows 95 TCP/IP stack.

4. You might need to also install any necessary SLIP connection software and write a connection script.

In this lesson you learned how to add CompuServe as a Mail service in Exchange and how to send and receive mail from the Internet and CompuServe. In the next lesson you will learn how to configure Exchange for your own preferences, how to create a personal profile, and how to add the Inbox to your Windows 95 Start Menu.

CREATING A PERSONAL PROFILE

In this lesson you will learn how to create a personal profile.

As you have learned, many different information services can be used within Exchange. Some of the information services are important to you if you travel or work from home in addition to working at an office location. Other information services are important if you use an online service such as The Microsoft Network or the Internet to transfer mail. These services are important to you, but not necessarily to other persons who may share your computer.

Creating personal profiles allows you to include those information services which apply to given situations. You might create a personal profile if you share your computer with other users. Or you might have one profile to use with your portable computer while traveling and another profile for when you connect your portable computer to your desktop computer while at the office. There might yet be another profile you use if your portable computer connects to an office network while you're using it at work.

Adding a personal profile is easy. Use these steps:

1. From the Windows desktop, click Start. Then select Settings, Control Panel.

2. Double-click Mail and Fax, then click Show Profiles. The Microsoft Exchange Profiles dialog box will appear.

3. Click Add. The Inbox Setup Wizard will begin, similar to Figure 21.1. All installed information services will appear on the information services list.

Figure 21.1   The Inbox Setup Wizard helps you create a personal profile.

4. Uncheck any services you do not want to include in your profile, then click Next.

5. You will be prompted to name your profile. Type a descriptive name for the profile. Use a name that will allow you to quickly identify what the purpose of the profile is. For example, you might name a profile "Away" if you plan to use it while traveling or at home, or "Office" for your office profile. Click Next to continue.

6. The Inbox Setup Wizard will now prompt you through the important settings necessary for the information services you have chosen. For example, if you have chosen to use Fax Services in your new profile, you will be prompted to select a fax modem, to select fax answering options, and to enter your name and fax number. Click Next at the bottom of each dialog box to continue to the next step in sequence.

7. When all information services have been configured, the Inbox Setup Wizard will ask whether you want to include the Inbox in your StartUp group. Click your choice, then click Next.

8. Click Finish to return to the Microsoft Exchange Profiles dialog box. Your new profile will be added to the list of available profiles.

9. If you want to automatically use your new profile when you start Exchange, select your new profile from the drop-down list under "When starting Microsoft Exchange, use this profile."

10. Click Close to return to the Windows desktop.

Step 9 in the previous series of steps only tells Exchange that your new profile should be the one listed in the Choose Profile dialog box each time you start Exchange. You'll still need to accept the profile or select an alternate one from the Choose Profile dialog box each time you start Exchange. Accept the listed profile by clicking OK. Or, to use an alternate profile, select one from the drop-down list in the Choose Profile dialog box, then select OK.

If you always want to select a certain profile each time you start Exchange by default (without prompting), use these steps:

1. From the Exchange Viewer, choose Tools, Options.

2. Click Always use this profile, then select your new profile from the drop-down list.

3. Click OK to return to the Exchange Viewer.

In this lesson you learned how to add, remove and rearrange columns which display in the Exchange Viewer, and how to create a personal profile. You also learned how to add the Inbox to your Windows 95 Startup group. In the next lesson you will learn how to customize the actions Exchange uses when you receive, send, and deliver mail. You will also learn how to set up network fax services.

LESSON 22

CUSTOMIZING MAIL AND FAX SERVICES

In this lesson you will learn how to customize the actions Exchange uses when you receive, send, and deliver Mail. You will also learn how to set up network Fax services.

As you continue to work with Exchange, you might find that you need to modify the actions used when messages are received, or when you send and deliver mail. For example, you might want a message to pop up on your screen whenever a new message is delivered to your Inbox. Or perhaps you want to allow other users to use your fax modem to send faxes. These actions, and many more, are designated by first displaying the Options dialog box, as shown in Figure 22.1. You should note that if Microsoft Office for Windows 95 is installed on your system, you'll have a tab to allow you to set Spelling options, also.

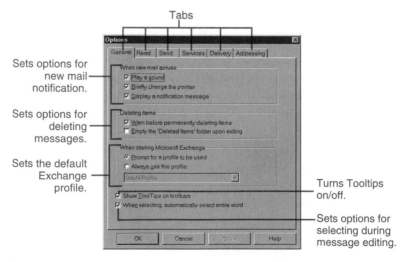

Tabs

Sets options for new mail notification.

Sets options for deleting messages.

Sets the default Exchange profile.

Turns Tooltips on/off.

Sets options for selecting during message editing.

FIGURE 22.1 The Options dialog box allows you to customize Exchange.

Using the General Tab

The General tab of the Options dialog box gathers several choices together that basically control any prompts you receive when using Exchange. The General tab (displayed in Figure 22.1) is the first to appear when you choose Tools, Options.

As listed below, the General tab allows you to set your preferences for mail receipt notification and whether you'll be warned before deleting messages. If desired, you can also set a default Exchange profile. You can also turn on or off tooltips display and set the action for selecting words when editing a message.

- **Customizing Mail Receipt Notification**   By default, when new mail is added to your Inbox, Exchange sounds a short "beep" and very briefly changes the current mouse pointer. A message icon will also be added to the clock area of your taskbar. But what if you're away from your computer when mail is received? You can instruct Exchange to display a small message dialog box on-screen notifying you of new messages by using the following steps. A sample notification message is shown in Figure 22.2.

Figure 22.2   Exchange can send you a new mail notification message.

1. From the Options dialog box, click the General tab if it's not already visible.

2. Check the Display a notification message checkbox.

3. If you are through setting options, click OK to return to the Exchange Viewer.

- **Setting Options for Deleting Messages**   You should delete those messages that are no longer needed on a regular basis. It is easy, however, to get carried away and delete messages by mistake. Exchange guards against this action by warning you when you delete messages from your Deleted Items folder. If you rarely, or never, make mistakes of this type, you can turn off this helpful message by removing the check from the Warn before permanently deleting items checkbox, as displayed in Figure 22.1.

As you delete messages from your personal folders, they are sent to the Deleted Items folder. Because messages can take up a lot of valuable disk space, you should be especially conscientious about emptying your Deleted Items folder when your personal folders are located on a network file server. You can instruct Exchange to empty the Deleted Items folder each time you exit by clicking the Empty the 'Deleted Items' folder upon exiting checkbox. Remember, however, that messages removed from the Deleted Items folder cannot be undeleted if you have removed them by mistake.

- **Setting a Default Exchange Profile**   As you learned in the previous lesson, you can create a personal profile. The General tab of the Options dialog box allows you to set that profile as a *default*. This means that Exchange will automatically start without prompting you to select a profile. To set a default profile, click the Always use this profile checkbox, then select the profile you want to use from the drop-down profile list.

USING THE READ TAB

The Read tab of the Options dialog box allows you to set your preferences when you read and reply to messages. Click the Read tab to view the options.

- **Setting Read Options When Moving or Deleting a Message**   After you have finished reading a mail message, it is a common practice to move the message to another folder (to keep your messages organized) or to delete the message. By setting actions in the Read tab, the next or previous message in your message list will open, or you will be returned to the Exchange Viewer. Click the choice you want to use from the "After moving or deleting an open item" area.

- **Setting Options for Replying or Forwarding a Message**   You can include all text from the original message when you compose a reply or forward a message. If you've chosen to include your original message text, you can also choose to indent that original text in the reply. In addition, your reply or comments can use alternate font settings.

To change the options you want to use when replying to a message, check the checkboxes in the "When replying to or forwarding an item" area of the Read tab. To change the font attributes, click the Font button to open the Font dialog box, then make any desired changes. When your font choices are complete, click OK to return to the Read tab. Then click OK again to return to the Exchange Viewer.

Using the Send Tab

The Send tab in the Options dialog box controls settings used when you compose and send a new message. Click the Send tab on the Options dialog box to set your new message options.

Check those options you want to use, uncheck those you don't need. When you're done choosing the options to use, click OK to return to the Exchange Viewer.

- **Setting a default message font**   You can change the default font used for the message text, including adding attributes such as underlining or strikeout. You can also assign a color to the text. Click the Font button, selecting those fonts and attributes you want to use. Then click OK to return to the Options dialog box.

- **Requesting receipts**   Requesting a receipt is especially useful if you use Fax services or online services for e-mail. When you've requested an "item delivered" receipt, a message is added to your Inbox which verifies that the fax or e-mail was successfully delivered. Similarly, receiving a "read" receipt for e-mail assures you that the message was delivered and read by the recipient. This is especially useful for e-mail delivered in your own office.

- **Setting sensitivity and importance levels**   Refer to Lesson 5 for more information on using these two message options. To modify the default sensitivity level for your message, select the level you want to use from the Set sensitivity drop-down list. Then click the Set importance option which best fits your normal message importance level.

- **Saving a copy of a sent message**   If you do not typically request a receipt for delivered or read messages, be sure that you, at least, keep a copy of the messages you send in your Sent Items folder. By doing so, you can send a lost message again, or even forward the message to another e-mail address.

Using the Services Tab

The Services tab is one method you can use to modify the properties for each information service associated with your profile. Remember that you can also modify service properties, or add new services by choosing Tools, Services. Each service included with your profile has individual settings, or *properties*.

Using the Services Tab Buttons

The Services tab uses five buttons to change or modify the services associated with the current profile. They are described in Table 22.1. To use each of the buttons (except for the Add button), first select the service by clicking the service name in the list, then click the button for the action you need. Refer to Table 22.1 for more information about the Add button.

Table 22.1   The buttons located on the Services tab

Button	Action
Add	Adds an installed service to the current profile. You can install a new service using the Mail and Fax choice in the Windows 95 Control Panel. Click the Add button, then select the service you want to add from the resulting list of installed services.
Remove	Removes a service from the current profile. Remove does not delete the service from your system.
Properties	Allows you to modify individual settings for the service you have selected. The Properties dialog box can also contain several tabs for service options. When you have finished making property changes, click OK to return to the Services tab.
Copy	Copies the selected service to another profile. You will see a list of profiles which reside on your computer. Select the profile you want to copy the service to, then click OK to return to the Services tab.
About	Lists all files associated with the selected service and describes them briefly. This is especially useful when you are troubleshooting a service that is not working properly.

Using the Delivery Tab

The Delivery tab in the Options dialog box sets a primary and secondary location for delivery of mail you receive. It also sets the order in which mail is delivered to the services in your profile.

- **Setting the primary and secondary folder
  locations**   The two drop-down lists, titled "Deliver new
  mail to the following location" and "Secondary location,"
  store the locations Exchange uses when it has mail to
  deliver to you. If you have not created a second set of
  personal folders, you will only have one possible location,
  designated as Personal Folders. If you have several sets of
  personal folders, you can tell Exchange exactly where to
  deliver your incoming mail. The secondary location is
  used only if the primary location is unavailable. For example, if your personal folders are located on your network drive and you are currently not working on the
  network, incoming mail could then be directed to a set of
  personal folders which exist on your personal hard drive.
  Review Lesson 10 for help in creating a new set of personal folders.

- **Processing Recipient addresses**   If you have more
  than one information service installed, such as Microsoft
  Mail and Microsoft Fax, messages will be delivered to
  those services in the order in which they are listed in the
  Information services list box. For example, messages waiting for delivery in the Outbox will first be delivered to
  any fax addresses, then Mail addresses, then MSN addresses, and finally to CompuServe Mail addresses. You
  can rearrange the delivery order by selecting a service and
  then clicking the up or down buttons to move the service
  up or down through the list.

When you have finished your Delivery option settings, click OK
to return to the Exchange Viewer.

USING THE ADDRESSING TAB

The Addressing tab in the Options dialog box allows you to
change the order in which Exchange searches and displays address books and the order in which address books are searched
when verifying an address. Click the Addressing tab to see the
dialog box.

- **Selecting the Address Book to be displayed first**   If you have more than one address book, it's really helpful to have your primary address book open first when you're looking for an address. From the "Show this address" drop-down list, select the address book you want to automatically open each time you start your address book.

"Keep personal addresses in" sets the address book you will use whenever you add addresses. Select the book you want to use from the drop-down list.

- **Changing the Order in which Addresses are Verified**   The Addressing tab sets the order addresses are checked when mail is delivered to each service. You can rearrange the order of address verification by selecting the list or book to be repositioned and then clicking the up or down arrow to move the book up or down in the list.

- **Changing the Filename Used for an Address Book**   A path and filename was associated with each address book at the time you installed Exchange and Microsoft Mail services. To change the address book location and filename:

    1. Select the address book to be modified.

    2. Click the Properties button.

    3. Change the path and filename for the address book by entering its location. If you're not sure of the location, click the Browse button to select it from the directory list.

    4. Click OK to return to the Addressing tab, then OK again to return to the Exchange Viewer.

In this lesson you learned how to customize the actions Exchange uses when you receive, send, and deliver Mail. You also learned how to set up network Fax services.

INSTALLING AND CONFIGURING EXCHANGE FOR REMOTE MAIL AND DIAL-UP NETWORKING

This Appendix will guide you through the benefits of using remote mail. You will learn how to install and configure Dial-Up Networking on both your office system and your portable system so that you can send and receive remote messages.

WHAT REMOTE MAIL AND DIAL-UP NETWORKING CAN DO FOR YOU

The *remote* mail capabilities of Exchange allow you to work away from your office computer. You can then dial into your office computer, or network using another computer equipped with a modem. This remote system may be a portable computer or perhaps a desktop computer at home. For purposes of this appendix, the remote system will be referred to as the *portable or remote computer.*

Remote mail will automatically pick up your messages, send messages that you have composed while offline, or even print a document or fax a message using equipment in your office. This is useful if you have a desktop system at work and a portable computer you use when away from your office. You can learn how to use Remote Mail in Lesson 18.

Both systems must be equipped with modems or fax modems. If you are communicating with a desktop system at work, both your remote system and your system at work must be configured for Windows 95. If you have not already done so, use the Windows 95 Control Panel (by selecting Start, Settings, Control Panel, then the Modems icon), to install and configure your modems for Windows 95. Similarly, if you're using a network with Exchange Server, the server modem must be properly configured to work with Windows NT.

SETTING UP YOUR SYSTEMS SO THAT YOU CAN PICK UP YOUR MAIL WHILE AWAY FROM THE OFFICE

Setting up remote mail and dial-up networking can be complex. If you are working on a network, you may need to ask your network administrator for assistance. If you are using Exchange Server, you will need to refer to your Exchange Server documentation for help installing and configuring Remote Mail and Dial-up Networking.

Using remote mail requires both a *client* system and a *server* system. The client system dials the server system to pick up messages. In other words, if you want to pick up messages from your office system using your portable computer, the portable is the *client* and your office system is the *server.*

The client portion of Dial-Up Networking is typically installed when you install Windows 95. The server, or host, portion is only available when you purchase and install the Dial-Up Server application from Microsoft Plus!, a Windows 95 companion program. You cannot set up the server or host computer which uses Windows 95 unless you purchase Microsoft Plus!.

INSTALLING THE SERVER SIDE OF DIAL-UP NETWORKING

The Server software should be installed on your computer at work. If you use a network, the server software is usually installed on the network server, although it does not necessarily have to be. To install the Dial-Up Networking Server, use these steps:

1. From the Windows 95 Control Panel, double-click Add/ Remove Programs, then click the Install/Uninstall tab and click Install. Windows 95 will prompt you to insert the installation floppy disk or CD-ROM.

2. Click Next when you have inserted the Plus! Setup floppy disk or CD-ROM into the drive. Windows 95 will then look for the Plus! setup file. When found, it will display the name and location of the installation file. The Plus! installation file is named SETUP.EXE. Click Finish to continue.

3. Click Add/Remove.

4. Click the Dial-Up Networking Server checkbox, then click Continue. See Figure A.1. All necessary files which allow your computer to act as a dial-up networking server will be copied to your system. You will then be prompted to restart your system. Click the Restart Windows button to do so.

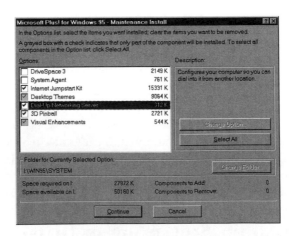

Figure A.1   Click the Dial-Up Networking Server choice from the Microsoft Plus! install window.

CONFIGURING THE DIAL-UP NETWORKING SERVER TO MONITOR INCOMING CALLS

Installing the Server software is only the first step. Next you must configure the software so that you will be able to access your system when you call from your portable or remote computer. Use these steps:

1. Open My Computer or the Explorer and double-click the Dial-Up Networking icon.

2. Choose Connections, then choose Dial-Up Server. The Dial-Up Server dialog box will appear as displayed in Figure A.2.

FIGURE A.2   The Dial-Up Server dialog box allows you to choose the users who can access your system.

3. Click Allow caller access.

4. Click Add. You will then be taken to a list of all users on your network.

5. Double-click your own name from the user list to add it to the list of persons who can dial-up your desktop computer. If you want to allow other users to dial-up your

computer, double-click their names also. When your list is complete, click OK.

Worried about security?   Unless your network is secured by Windows NT or Novell Netware security procedures, be cautious about allowing other users to dial-up your computer since doing so opens up the entire network to them. You should discuss security issues with your system administrator before adding other users to your dial-up networking list!

6. Click OK again. This sets the status of your system to monitor for incoming calls and closes the Dial-Up Server dialog box.

INSTALLING THE CLIENT SIDE OF DIAL-UP NETWORKING

Next, you need to verify if you have the Dial-Up Networking client portion of Windows 95 installed on your portable system. To do so, on your portable, open My Computer or the Windows 95 Explorer. Dial-Up Networking will appear if installed. If Dial-Up Networking is not installed on your portable system, use these steps:

1. Insert the Windows 95 installation disk in your portable's disk drive.

2. Click on the Start button and select Settings, Control Panel, double-click Add/Remove Programs, then click the Windows Setup tab.

3. Click Communications, then click the Details button.

4. Click the Dial-Up Networking checkbox, then click OK.

You will be returned to the Windows Setup dialog box.

5. Click OK. The Dial-Up Networking client files will be copied to your portable. When complete, you will be prompted to restart your computer.

6. Click OK, then OK again to restart the computer.

CONFIGURING THE CLIENT SIDE OF DIAL-UP NETWORKING

Now that you have verified that the client software is installed on your portable, you must configure it to dial your computer at work. To do so:

1. Open My Computer or the Windows 95 Explorer and double-click the Dial-Up Networking icon. The Dial-Up Networking list will appear.

2. Double-click the Make New Connection icon, or choose Connections, Make New Connection. The Make New Connection dialog box will appear, as displayed in Figure A.3.

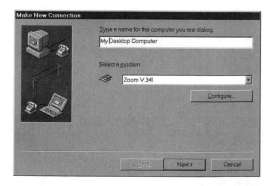

FIGURE A.3   New Dial-Up Connections are named in the Make New Connection dialog box.

3. Type a name you will recognize when you use Dial-Up Networking. You might want to name your connection something like "My Desktop Computer."

4. If you have multiple modems available, be sure to also select your modem from the drop-down modem list. Then, if necessary, configure the modem by clicking the Configure button and making any changes you require. Click OK when finished to return to the Make New Connection dialog box.

5. Click Next to continue.

6. Type the area code and phone number you will use when dialing your computer at work. Click Next when the numbers are correct.

7. Click Finish to close the Dial-Up Networking Wizard. A new icon will appear in your Dial-Up Networking list.

The Dial-Up Adapter is not configured! If a Dial-Up Adapter was not previously configured or installed, the Dial-Up Networking Wizard will continue. Complete the configuration steps.

Configuring Exchange on Your Portable Computer for Remote Messaging

The last step in setting up your portable computer is to tell Exchange how to dial your system at work and any preferences you have for sending and receiving remote mail.

Identifying Your Postoffice to Exchange for Remote Messaging

Use these steps to configure Exchange for remote messaging:

1. On your portable computer, start Exchange.

2. Now choose Tools, Services.

3. Select Microsoft Mail, then click Properties. The Microsoft Mail dialog box will appear as displayed in Figure A.4.

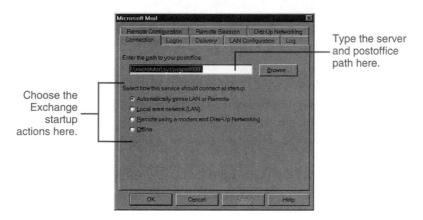

Type the server and postoffice path here.

Choose the Exchange startup actions here.

FIGURE A.4   The Connection tab identifies your Mail postoffice.

4. In the Enter the path to your postoffice text box, type the Universal Naming Convention (UNC) to your Microsoft Mail postoffice. A UNC indicates that the path resides on a remote computer and starts with two backslashes, as in **\\server\wgpo0000**.

5. Click the Exchange startup option you want to use, then click OK. You will be returned to the Services dialog box.

6. Click OK to return to the Exchange Viewer.

CHOOSING A DIAL-UP NETWORKING CONNECTION

Next you must tell Exchange which connection to use:

1. From within the Microsoft Mail Properties dialog box (follow steps 1-3 above), click the Dial-Up Networking tab.

2. Select the connection you will use when dialing your work computer for messaging from the drop-down connection list.

3. Click any other options you want to use, such as setting a number of times the modem should retry the connection if it fails, and whether a Dial-Up Networking session should be confirmed. Then click OK. You will be returned to the Services dialog box.

4. Click OK to return to the Exchange Viewer.

Setting Options for Retrieving and Sending Mail Remotely

Options can be set which will force Dial-Up Networking when Exchange is started, or which control whether you remain *online* while all mail is transferred to your portable system. To set your remote mail preferences:

1. From the Microsoft Mail Properties dialog box, click the Remote Session tab.

2. Make any option choices you desire, then click OK. You will be returned to the Services dialog box.

3. Click OK to return to the Exchange Viewer.

4. Exit Exchange by choosing File, Exit, then restart Exchange normally. This will cause your remote mail configuration to take effect.

WINDOWS 95 PRIMER

B

*Microsoft Windows 95 is a graphical
operating system that makes your
computer easy to use by providing menus and pictures
to select. Before you can take advantage of it, however, you
must learn some Windows 95 basics.*

A FIRST LOOK AT WINDOWS 95

You don't have to start Windows 95—it starts automatically when
you turn on your PC. After the initial startup screens, you arrive
at a screen something like the one shown in Figure B.1. (Notice
how the open programs look on the Taskbar in Figure B.1.)

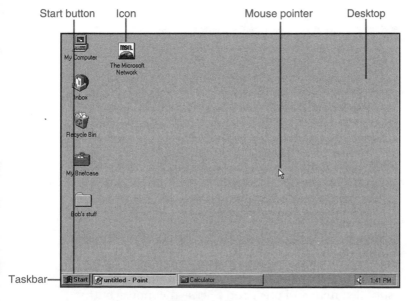

FIGURE B.1 The Windows 95 screen.

Parts of the Screen

As shown in Figure B.1, the Windows 95 screen contains many special elements and controls. Here's a brief summary:

- The background on which all the pictures and boxes rest is the *desktop*.

- The *Taskbar* shows the windows and programs that are open. You can switch between open windows and programs by clicking the name on the Taskbar.

- The *Start button* opens a menu system from which you can start programs. Click on the Start button; then, click on your selection from each menu that appears.

- Some *icons* appear on your desktop—you can activate one by double-clicking on it.

You'll learn more about these elements as we continue.

 Also Appearing... If your computer has Microsoft Office installed on it, you see the Office Shortcuts toolbar on-screen too. It's a series of little pictures strung together horizontally, representing Office programs. Hold the mouse over a picture to see what it does; click on it to launch the program. See your Microsoft Office documentation to learn more.

Using a Mouse

To work most efficiently in Windows, you need a mouse. Here are the mouse actions you need to know:

- *Point* means to move the mouse pointer onto the specified item by moving the mouse. The tip of the mouse pointer must touch the item.

- *Click* on an item means to move the pointer onto the specified item and press and release the mouse button once. Unless specified otherwise (i.e., right-click), use the left mouse button. Clicking usually selects an item.

- *Double-click* on an item means to move the pointer to the specified item and press and release the left mouse button twice quickly. Double-clicking usually activates an item.

- *Drag* means to move the mouse pointer onto the item, hold down the mouse button, and move the mouse while holding down the button. Unless specified (i.e., right-drag), use the left mouse button.

CONTROLLING A WINDOW WITH THE MOUSE

Windows are the heart of the Windows 95 program. Windows 95 sections off these rectangular areas for particular purposes, such as running a program. You can control a window using the procedures shown in Figure B.2.

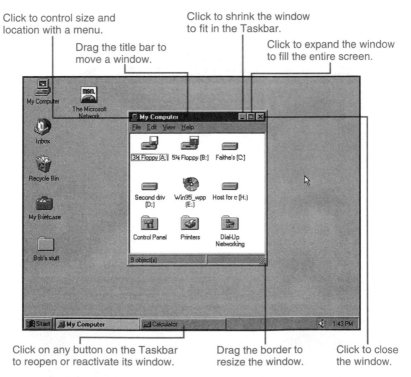

Click to control size and location with a menu.

Click to shrink the window to fit in the Taskbar.

Drag the title bar to move a window.

Click to expand the window to fill the entire screen.

Click on any button on the Taskbar to reopen or reactivate its window.

Drag the border to resize the window.

Click to close the window.

FIGURE B.2 Use your mouse to control windows.

Scroll Bars   If your window contains more icons than it can display at once, scroll bars appear on the bottom and/or right edges of the window. To move through the window's contents, click on an arrow button at either end of a scroll bar to move in that direction, or drag the gray bar in the direction you want to move.

GETTING HELP

Windows 95 comes with a great on-line Help system. To access it, click your mouse on the Start button, and click on Help. You see the box shown in Figure B.3.

FIGURE B.3   Windows offers several kinds of help.

There are three tabs in this box: Contents, Index, and Find. The Contents tab appears on top first. To move to a tab, click on it. Here's how to use each tab:

- Contents   Double-click on any book to open it. Sub-books and documents appear. Double-click on sub-books and documents to open them.

- Index   Type the word you want to look up. The Index list scrolls to that part of the alphabetical listing. When you see the topic on the list that you want to read, double-click on it.

- Find   The first time you click on this tab, Windows tells you it needs to create a list. Click Next, and Finish to allow this. Then you see the main Find tab. Type the word you want to find in the top text box. Then click a word in the middle box to narrow the search. Finally, review the list of help topics at the bottom, and double-click the one you want to read.

When you're done reading about a document, click Help Topics to return to the main Help screen, or click Back to return to the previous Help topic. Or, click the window's Close button to exit Help.

STARTING A PROGRAM

There are many ways to start a program, but here is the simplest (see Figure B.4):

1. Click the Start button.

2. Click Programs.

3. Click on the group that contains the program you want to start (for instance, Microsoft Office 95).

4. Click on the program you want to start (for instance, Microsoft Access).

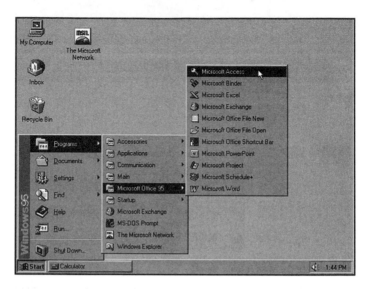

Figure B.4   Click on the Start button; then, click on each menu and submenu, until you find the program you want to start.

Another way to start a program is to open a document that you created in that program—the program automatically opens when the document opens. Double-click on a document file in My Computer or Windows Explorer to open it, or click the Start button and select a recently-used document from the Documents menu.

You can also start a program by double-clicking on its shortcut icon on the desktop. Shortcut icons are links to other files. When you use a shortcut, Windows simply follows the link back to the original file.

Whenever you use a document or program frequently, you might consider creating a shortcut for it on the desktop. To do so, just use the right mouse button to drag an object out of Windows Explorer or My Computer. On the shortcut menu that appears, select Create Shortcut(s) Here.

USING MENUS

Almost all Windows programs have menu bars containing menus. The menu names appear across the top of the screen in a row. To open a menu, click on its name. The menu drops down, displaying its commands. To select a command, click on it.

 Shortcut Keys Notice in Figure B.5 that key names, such as Enter for the Open command or F8 for the Copy command, appear after some command names. These are shortcut keys. You use these keys to perform the commands without opening the menu.

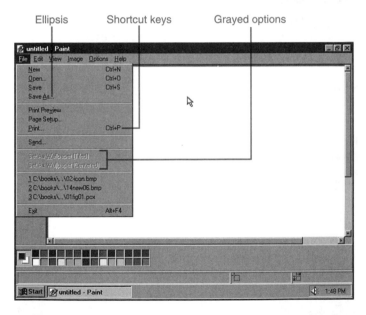

FIGURE B.5 A menu lists various commands you can perform.

Usually, when you select a command, Windows 95 executes the command immediately. However:

- If the command name is gray (instead of black), the command is unavailable at the moment and you cannot choose it.

- If the command name is followed by an arrow, as with the Start button's menus, selecting the command causes another menu to appear, from which you must make another selection.

- If the command is followed by an ellipsis (three dots), selecting it will cause a dialog box to appear. You'll learn about dialog boxes in the next section.

Using Shortcut Menus

A new feature in Windows 95 is the shortcut menu. Right-click on any object (any icon, screen element, file or folder, etc.), and a shortcut menu appears, as shown in Figure B.6. The shortcut menu contains commands that apply only to the selected object. Click on any command to select it, or click outside the menu to cancel.

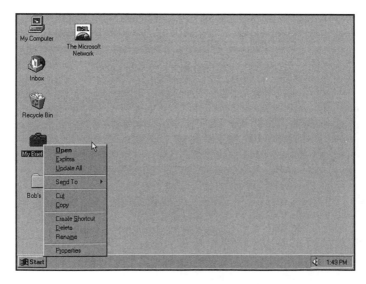

Figure B.6   Shortcut menus are new for Windows 95.

NAVIGATING DIALOG BOXES

A dialog box is the operating system's way of requesting additional information. For example, if you choose Print from the File menu of the WordPad application, you see a dialog box something like the one shown in Figure B.7. (Its exact look will vary depending on your printer.)

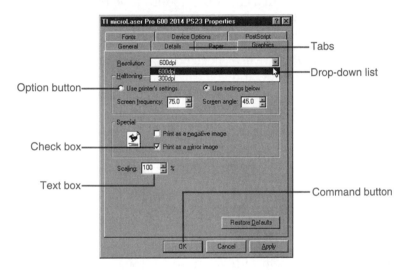

FIGURE B.7   A dialog box requests additional information.

Each dialog box contains one or more of the following elements:

- *Tabs* bring up additional "pages" of options you can choose. Click on a tab to activate it.

- *List boxes* display available choices. Click on any item on the list to select it. If the entire list is not visible, use the scroll bar to find additional choices.

- *Drop-down lists* are similar to list boxes, but only one item in the list is shown. To see the rest of the list, click the down arrow to the right of the list box. Then click on an item to select it.

- *Text boxes* enable you to type in an entry. Just click inside the text box and type. Text boxes that expect numeric input usually have up and down arrow buttons (increment buttons) that let you bump the number up and down.

- *Check boxes* enable you to turn on or off an individual option. Click on a check box to turn it on or off. Each check box is an independent unit that doesn't affect other check boxes.

- *Option buttons* are like check boxes, but option buttons appear in groups, and you can select only one. When you select an option button, PowerPoint deselects any others you already selected. Click on a button to activate it.

- *Command buttons* perform an action, such as executing the options you set, closing the dialog box, or opening another dialog box. To select a command button, click on it.

From Here...

If you need more help with Windows 95, I suggest one of these books:

The Complete Idiot's Guide to Windows 95 by Paul McFedries

Windows 95 Cheat Sheet by Joe Kraynak

The Big Basics Book of Windows 95 by Shelley O'Hara, Jennifer Fulton, and Ed Guilford

INDEX

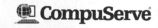

Complete and Return this Card
for a *FREE* Computer Book Catalog

Thank you for purchasing this book! You have purchased a superior computer book written expressly for your needs. To continue to provide the kind of up-to-date, pertinent coverage you've come to expect from us, we need to hear from you. Please take a minute to complete and return this self-addressed, postage-paid form. In return, we'll send you a free catalog of all our computer books on topics ranging from word processing to programming and the internet.

r. ☐   Mrs. ☐   Ms. ☐   Dr. ☐

ame (first) ☐☐☐☐☐☐☐☐☐☐ (M.I.) ☐ (last) ☐☐☐☐☐☐☐☐☐☐☐☐☐☐☐

ddress ☐☐☐☐☐☐☐☐☐☐☐☐☐☐☐☐☐☐☐☐☐☐☐☐☐☐☐☐

☐☐☐☐☐☐☐☐☐☐☐☐☐☐☐☐☐☐☐☐☐☐☐☐☐☐☐☐

ty ☐☐☐☐☐☐☐☐☐☐☐☐☐ State ☐☐ Zip ☐☐☐☐☐ ☐☐☐☐

one ☐☐☐ ☐☐☐ ☐☐☐☐   Fax ☐☐☐ ☐☐☐ ☐☐☐☐

mpany Name ☐☐☐☐☐☐☐☐☐☐☐☐☐☐☐☐☐☐☐☐☐☐☐☐☐

mail address ☐☐☐☐☐☐☐☐☐☐☐☐☐☐☐☐☐☐☐☐☐☐☐☐☐☐☐☐

. Please check at least (3) influencing factors for purchasing this book.

ront or back cover information on book .... ☐
pecial approach to the content .... ☐
ompleteness of content .... ☐
uthor's reputation .... ☐
ublisher's reputation .... ☐
ook cover design or layout .... ☐
ndex or table of contents of book .... ☐
rice of book .... ☐
pecial effects, graphics, illustrations .... ☐
ther (Please specify): _____ ☐

. How did you first learn about this book?

nternet Site .... ☐
aw in Macmillan Computer
    Publishing catalog .... ☐
ecommended by store personnel .... ☐
aw the book on bookshelf at store .... ☐
ecommended by a friend .... ☐
eceived advertisement in the mail .... ☐
aw an advertisement in: _____ ☐
ead book review in: _____ ☐
ther (Please specify): _____ ☐

. How many computer books have you purchased in the last six months?

his book only .... ☐   3 to 5 books .... ☐
 books .... ☐   More than 5 .... ☐

4. Where did you purchase this book?

Bookstore .... ☐
Computer Store .... ☐
Consumer Electronics Store .... ☐
Department Store .... ☐
Office Club .... ☐
Warehouse Club .... ☐
Mail Order .... ☐
Direct from Publisher .... ☐
Internet site .... ☐
Other (Please specify): .... ☐

5. How long have you been using a computer?

Less than 6 months .. ☐   6 months to a year ..... ☐
1 to 3 years .... ☐   More than 3 years ...... ☐

6. What is your level of experience with personal computers and with the subject of this book?

	With PC's	With subject of book
New	☐	☐
Casual	☐	☐
Accomplished	☐	☐
Expert	☐	☐

Source Code — ISBN: 0-7897-0677-6

7. Which of the following best describes your job title?

Administrative Assistant .... ☐
Coordinator .... ☐
Manager/Supervisor .... ☐
Director .... ☐
Vice President .... ☐
President/CEO/COO .... ☐
Lawyer/Doctor/Medical Professional .... ☐
Teacher/Educator/Trainer .... ☐
Engineer/Technician .... ☐
Consultant .... ☐
Not employed/Student/Retired .... ☐
Other (Please specify): .... ☐

8. Which of the following best describes the area of the company your job title falls under?

Accounting .... ☐
Engineering .... ☐
Manufacturing .... ☐
Marketing .... ☐
Operations .... ☐
Sales .... ☐
Other (Please specify): .... ☐

9. What is your age?

Under 20 .... ☐
21-29 .... ☐
30-39 .... ☐
40-49 .... ☐
50-59 .... ☐
60-over .... ☐

10. Are you:

Male .... ☐
Female .... ☐

11. Which computer publications do you read regularly? (Please list)

_____
_____
_____
_____
_____
_____
_____
_____
_____
_____
_____

Comments: _____
_____
_____

Fold here and scotch-tape to